D0925218

DEVIOUS DEDUCTIONS

DEVIOUS DEDUCTIONS

METRO BOOKS
NEW YORK

All puzzles, artwork, text and collection © 2005 Book Creation Ltd.

This 2009 edition published by Metro Books,
by arrangement with Book Creation, LLC.

All rights reserved. No part of this publication may be reproduced, stored in a retrieval system,
or transmitted, in any form or by any means, electronic, mechanical, photocopying, recording,
or otherwise, without prior written permission from the copyright holder.

Detailed acknowledgements appear on page 128.

Metro Books
122 Fifth Avenue
New York, NY 10011

ISBN 978-1-4351-1751-8

Printed and bound in China

10 9 8 7 6 5 4 3 2 1

Devious Deductions is a brand-new volume of puzzles for those who love to pit their wits against a succession of math and logic problems until the right answers can be found.

But what is deduction? This is a word that brings to mind immediately the abilities of great fictional detectives, such as Sherlock Holmes, or perhaps famous mathematicians working together to find a secret formula. But we often miss the part deduction plays in our everyday lives. We continually draw conclusions from any problem at hand and use the facts at our disposal to arrive at a solution.

In the same way, that's how we arrive at an answer to a puzzle. With familiar questions we might be able to use tried-and-tested methods on the path to the answer. At every dead end we take one or several steps back until we reach the point of security, where we knew our reasoning to be sound. This might be halfway through a puzzle or it might mean going back to the start. It can be frustrating but it is important never to give up, as you may find the answer only after you have exhausted every possibility. Each puzzle you try builds on your ability to solve the next one because of the deductive skills you have gathered from your previous attempts. No puzzle in this book is so tough that it is unsolvable, but quite a few will give you a good run for your money!

You'll also find that you will build your deductive powers of inference—i.e., your ability to find the solution based solely on the facts put before you.

Probably the most famous advocate of this method is Sherlock Holmes. He believed that he needed to know nothing but that which could be observed to solve the case at hand. From this process of observation and deduction he could "distinguish the history of a man, and the trade or profession to which he belongs," from his appearance. Pushing this idea further, he noted that "from a drop of water, a logician could infer the possibility of an Atlantic or Niagara without having seen or heard of one or the other."

But even the greatest detective can be fooled, a commonsense approach finding only the best explanation available among many alternatives. We hope, however, that these puzzles are within your grasp. In developing your own process of deduction into a finely honed process, you'll find that the answer is sometimes immediately forthcoming—much like the easier questions in this book. Other puzzles require a new way of looking, and here logic and perspective combine to give the outcome.

In this respect we've been kind. We know that some puzzles take longer than others to fathom, so we've given them time ratings. Difficult puzzles—indicated by the star ratings—are allocated more solving time than others.

These puzzles will help develop the left side of your brain—the part affiliated with logic, reasoning, and number skills. Perhaps you didn't realize it, but one human activity that demonstrates our natural propensity to deduction is the process of resolving an argument. Now, I hope there'll be no arguments over this book—apart from, of course, whose turn it is to try the next puzzle! ✪

—David Popey

1 DIFFICULTY ★★★★★☆☆☆☆☆  Minutes

Can you navigate this maze, never retracing your steps, and collecting just one of each of the digits 1 to 9 along the way?

Start here

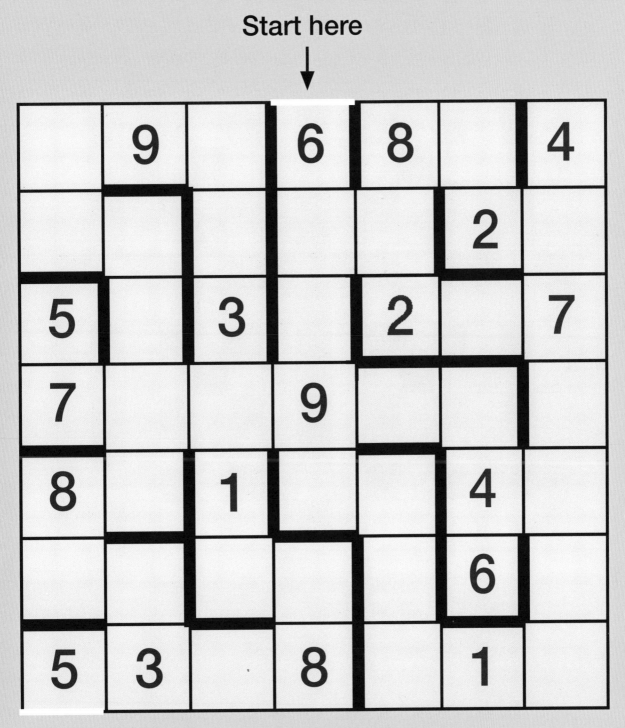

Finish

2 DIFFICULTY ✪✪✪✪✪✪✪✪✪✪  **6** Minutes

Can you fit these numbers into the grid? One number has already been inserted to help you get started.

3 Digits	4 Digits	5 Digits	~~87396~~	7 Digits	6497834
176	1475	18839	90582	1753884	7320620
383	2366	28296		1976487	7635841
657	3937	39597	6 Digits	2733264	8602330
791	5243	43187	363608	3960316	8944694
873	6562	58354	415676	4994676	9740926
946	7265	62206	502796	5160060	
	8267	66517	792521	5169430	
	9123	74945		6394615	

3 DIFFICULTY ✪✪✪✪✪✪✪✩✩✩

 **Minutes**

Five guests mislaid items in their hotel rooms following a wild weekend. Can you figure out who left what in which room of which hotel?

	Geoffrey	Rupert	Gerald	Maria	Caroline	Hilton	Novotel	Travelodge	Royal	Westin	Glasses	Camera	Watch	Alarm clock	Umbrella
2															
21															
33															
50															
65															
Glasses															
Camera															
Watch															
Alarm clock															
Umbrella															
Hilton															
Novotel															
Travelodge															
Royal															
Westin															

1. Geoffrey left his umbrella at the Hilton.
2. Maria lost her alarm clock. Her room number was higher than 30.
3. The Royal's highest numbered room is 20, and they didn't find a camera.
4. Rupert was in room 33; he doesn't wear glasses.
5. The watch found belonged to a woman and wasn't found at the Novotel.
6. Caroline's room number was higher than Maria's. Neither woman stayed at the Travelodge.

4 DIFFICULTY ✪✪✪✪✪✩✩✩✩✩

 **Minutes**

Make a calculation totaling the figure on the right by inserting the four mathematical signs (+, −, ÷, x) between the numbers shown.

They can be in any order, and one of them has been used twice.

8		4		9		2		6		7	=	9

5 DIFFICULTY ✪✪✪✪✪✪✪✪✪✪ **5** Minutes

Given that scales a and b balance perfectly, how many spoons are needed to balance scale c?

6 DIFFICULTY ✪✪✪✪✪✪✪✪✪✪ — ⏱ **8** Minutes

Fill in the grid so that every row, every column, and every 3 x 3 box contains the numbers 1 to 9.

2			5		4			6
				3			4	5
			1		7	2	3	8
5		4	7		9	3		
	1					5	8	9
6		9	8			4	2	7
		1	4	9	3			
	4	6		7	1			3
3	2	7		5			9	

7 DIFFICULTY ✪✪✪✪✪✪✪✪✪✪ — ⏱ **4** Minutes

The four animals each represent a number between 1 and 4. If a cat is worth 3, can you figure out the correct values of the other animals in order to make a successful sum?

+

+

+

+

───────────────

=

8 DIFFICULTY ✪✪✪✪✪✪☆☆☆☆  **4** Minutes

The number 234,567 appears just once in this number-search grid and occurs in a straight line, running either backward or forward in a horizontal, vertical, or diagonal direction. Can you find it?

2	3	2	7	7	2	7	2	5	4	3	2
7	3	4	2	3	4	6	5	7	3	3	7
2	7	2	4	2	5	6	7	2	4	4	2
2	3	5	5	3	3	6	5	5	7	3	7
2	5	2	4	4	4	4	7	4	4	3	6
7	3	7	5	3	3	2	5	5	3	2	5
6	5	6	2	2	2	3	7	6	4	2	4
5	7	3	2	3	3	6	6	3	6	3	3
3	2	5	5	3	4	2	5	5	2	5	2
4	5	4	4	5	6	5	4	4	4	4	2
2	3	7	5	3	7	3	6	2	3	3	7
2	3	4	5	6	2	7	3	2	7	2	2

9 DIFFICULTY ✪✪✪✪✪✪✪✪✪✪  **4** Minutes

Every row and column contains the same numbers and signs, but they are arranged in a different order each time. Find the correct order to arrive at the final totals shown.

4	X	5	−	8	+	2	= 14
						=	13
						=	20
						=	17
=		=		=		=	
29		24		30		6	

10 DIFFICULTY ✪✪✪✪✩✩✩✩✩✩  Minutes

Which of the four boxed figures (a, b, c, or d) completes the set?

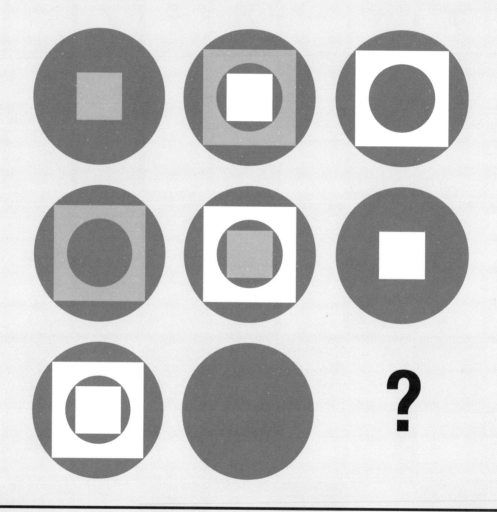

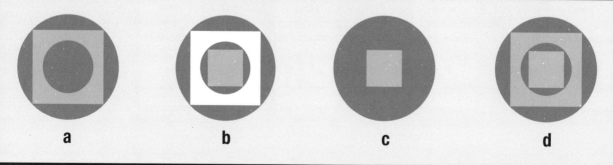

a   b   c   d

11 DIFFICULTY ✪✪✪✪✪✪✪✪✪✪

 **6** Minutes

Can you fit these numbers into the grid? One number has already been inserted to help you get started.

3 Digits	4 Digits	5 Digits	83717	7 Digits	6656542
189	1214	11632	96219	1015828	7794120
329	2503	29491		1518426	8413195
431	3064	31472	**6 Digits**	2474142	8543365
504	4092	49056	151371	2503811	9262593
784	5403	51594	335283	3790656	9638691
839	6879	58035	502921	4560356	
	7397	69795	801384	5414585	
	8541	70263		5942029	

12 DIFFICULTY ✪✪✪✪✪✪✪✪✪✪ ③ Minutes

Which is the odd number out?

78419   43916

96823   87924

24714   83617

13 DIFFICULTY ✪✪✪✪✪✪✪✪✪✪ ⑤ Minutes

is to:

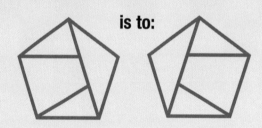

as

is to:

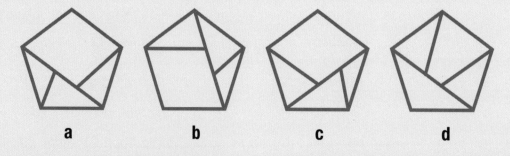

a   b   c   d

14 DIFFICULTY ✪✪✪✪✪✪✪✪✪✪  Minutes

Make a calculation totaling the figure on the right by inserting the four mathematical signs (+, −, ÷, x) between the numbers shown.

They can be inserted in any order, and one of them has been used twice.

| 5 | | 4 | | 2 | | 8 | | 6 | | 3 | = | 5 |

15 DIFFICULTY ✪✪✪✪✪✪✪✪✪✪  Minutes

Fill in the grid so that every row, every column, and every 3 x 3 box contains the numbers 1 to 9.

		8	5	4	9			
	9	3			7		8	
4	1	5		8		9		
3			7		6			4
5		1			8		9	3
7	4		3	5			2	
		6				2	4	1
	2			6	4	3	5	
			9	3		6		8

16 DIFFICULTY ✪✪✪✪✪☆☆☆☆☆

 **Minutes**

Five people took part in five different events at the county fair in Minton, Delaware. Can you name each competitor and match them to the event they entered, how they did, and where the event was held?

	McClusky	Grady	Smith	Denton	Carlisle	1st	2nd	3rd	4th	5th	Barn	Yard	Meadow	Church house	Town square	Hog tie	Pie eating	Lasso	Pumpkin throwing	Line dancing
Zak																				
Shooter																					
Amy																					
Betty Lou																					
Johnny																					
Hog tie																					
Pie eating																				
Lasso																				
Pumpkin throwing																				
Line dancing																				
Barn																				
Yard																				
Meadow																				
Church house																				
Town square																				
1st																				
2nd																				
3rd																				
4th																				
5th																				

1. Zak Carlisle was in the hog-tie event. There were only three competitors and it wasn't held in the meadow.
2. The third-place finisher in the church house wasn't a woman.
3. The fourth-place finisher in the lasso contest wasn't a woman or a Grady.
4. The pie-eating winner wasn't a Grady either, and placed higher than the pumpkin thrower.
5. The pie-eating competiton wasn't in the barn or the church house.
6. Amy was in the yard. Smith and Carlisle were not.
7. Betty Lou McClusky didn't win her event, which wasn't lasso, nor was it held in the barn.
8. Shooter came first, but not in the hog-tie or pie-eating events, and not in the barn or church house.
9. The pumpkin-throwing event was held in the town square, and was entered by one of the two women.

17 DIFFICULTY ✪✪✪✪✪✪✪✪✩✩

8 Minutes

The number 45,678,123 appears twice in this number-search grid and occurs in a diamond shape, running in an counterclockwise direction, but not starting in any particular square, similar to the example shown here.
Can you locate both instances?

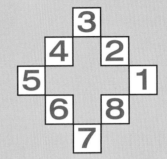

8	1	1	4	3	8	7	5	4	1	2	6	1	1	3
1	8	2	2	3	2	1	6	2	7	8	1	2	8	8
5	1	3	1	1	3	1	2	5	5	2	3	2	1	4
1	4	2	8	7	2	3	4	3	3	1	3	1	3	6
2	3	6	4	8	6	3	4	8	2	4	3	4	5	1
4	6	3	7	6	1	5	1	2	1	4	5	2	6	1
5	5	1	7	2	5	2	3	2	1	8	4	6	1	5
8	8	6	7	1	2	4	3	2	4	3	7	2	6	8
1	1	1	3	6	1	4	3	4	2	6	8	1	5	7
3	4	2	6	4	5	7	5	1	5	7	2	4	1	8
2	1	1	3	8	5	6	4	3	8	6	1	3	3	2
8	6	8	7	6	7	4	8	1	8	7	5	4	1	3
1	8	6	1	5	3	1	2	7	1	1	6	1	4	2
3	8	2	4	8	1	1	8	3	8	5	2	2	1	6
1	3	7	6	2	2	8	8	6	4	3	1	2	3	4

18 DIFFICULTY ✪✪✪✪☆☆☆☆☆☆

Each row and column contains the same numbers and signs, but they are arranged in a different order each time. Find the correct order to arrive at the final totals shown.

4	x	3	−	6	+	2	=	8
							=	18
							=	14
							=	19
=		=		=		=		
5		2		28		11		

19 DIFFICULTY ✪✩✪✪✪✪✩✪✩✪✪   **4** Minutes

Which of the four boxed figures (a, b, c, or d) completes the set?

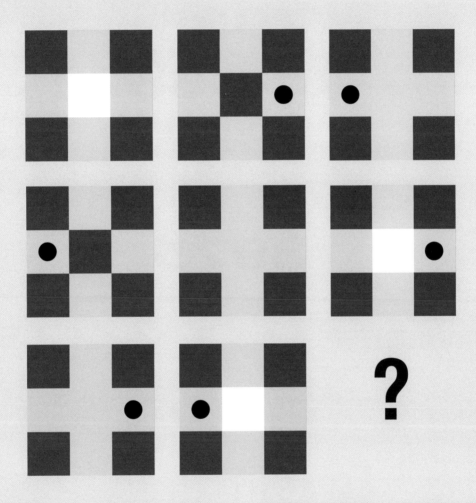

?

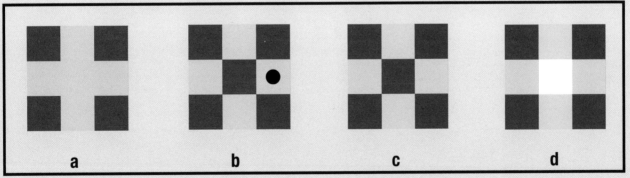

a   b   c   d

20 DIFFICULTY ✪✪✪✪✪✪☆☆☆☆  3 Minutes

Which number is the odd one out?

9364   5973
7935
7851   6872
1857
2876   4369
3975

21 DIFFICULTY ✪✪✪✪✪✪☆☆☆☆ 4 Minutes

Which of the groups of numbers below (a, b, c, or d) is the missing section of the grid?

10	13	12	15
11	14		16
8	11		13
9	12	11	

a 15
   12
      16

b 13
   10
      14

c 13
   12
      14

d 10
   15
      16

22 DIFFICULTY ✪✪✪✪✪✪✪✪✪✪  4 Minutes

What number should replace the question mark in this sequence?

1000 989 976 961 ? 925 904

23 DIFFICULTY ✪✪✪✪✪✪✪✪✪✪  10 Minutes

Five chefs prepare their specialty dessert for five fashionable restaurants.
Can you match each cook to a dish and a restaurant?

1. Gavin made a crumble for Tables.
2. The chocolate dish was for Delish, and it wasn't a tart or a cake.
3. The apple pie wasn't made by a woman, but the cake was.
4. Pierre made the banana dish, but not for YumYum or Din.
5. The rhubarb dish was made for Din, but not by Sally.

	Pierre	Gavin	Sally	Rachel	Arthur	Pie	Cake	Tart	Souffle	Crumble	Apple	Rhubarb	Cherry	Chocolate	Banana
Delish															
Resto															
YumYum															
Tables															
Din															
Pie															
Cake															
Tart															
Souffle															
Crumble															
Apple															
Rhubarb															
Cherry															
Chocolate															
Banana															

24 DIFFICULTY ✪✪✪✪✪✪✪✪✪✪  Minutes

Start your journey from the exact center of the maze, moving from die to die (it is up to you to figure out a system, but you must visit every die). You have completed the maze when you have found which die is the last on your journey.

The colors give a clue to your direction of travel.

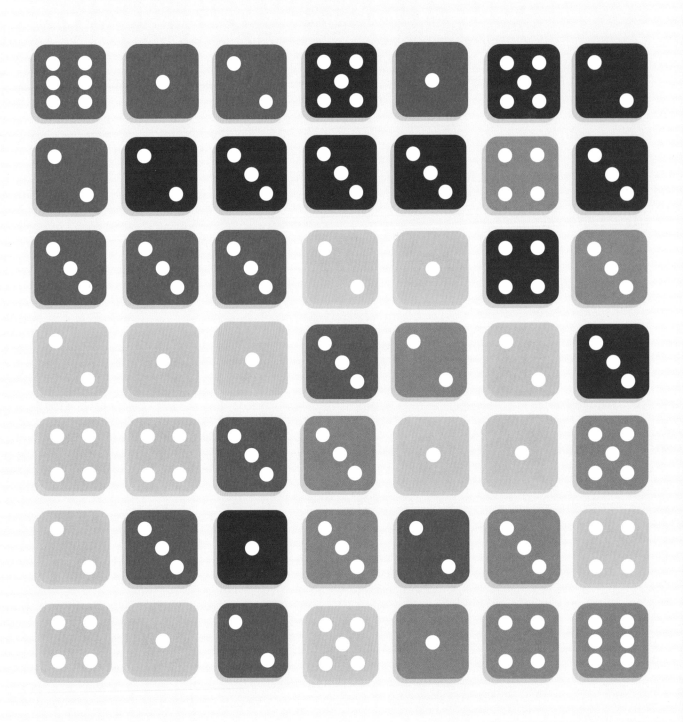

25 DIFFICULTY ✪✪✪✪✪✪✪✪✪✪

20 Minutes

Complete this number grid and you'll be a roaring success.

How to do a number grid:
Along each row or column are numbers that indicate how many blocks of black squares are in a line. For example, "3, 4, 5" indicates that from left to right or top to bottom there is a group of three black squares, then a group of four black squares, then a group of five black squares. Each block of black squares on the same line must have at least one white square between it and the next block of squares. Blocks of black squares may or may not have a number of white squares before or after them. It is sometimes possible to determine which squares will be black without reference to other lines or columns. It is helpful to put a small dot in a square you know will be empty.

26 DIFFICULTY ✪✪✪✪✪✪☆☆☆  **6** Minutes

Can you crack the safe? First decide which of the 14 statements given are false. Then shade out the areas on the combination lock that are labeled with the letters of those false statements (so if you think statement A is false, shade out area A). The remaining lit segments will give you the digital combination required.

Hint: five of the statements are false.

A.   The word "rotavator" is a palindrome.
B.   Rossini composed the opera *Carmen.*
C.   Dividing by a half is the same as multiplying by two.
D.   The currency of Portugal is the escudo.
E.   The Romans fitted glass into some of their windows.
F.   Mount McKinley is the highest point in North America.
G.   A dystopia is an unpleasant imaginary world.
H.   The artist El Greco was born in the 16th century.
I.   George W. Bush is the 42nd President of the United States.
J.   All Saints' Day occurs on November 1.
K.   In the game of poker, a straight beats a flush.
L.   The three major deities of Hinduism are Brahma, Shiva, and Vishnu.
M.   Chalk consists of the chemical calcium carbonate.
N.   The 1998 Winter Olympics were held in Nagano, South Korea.

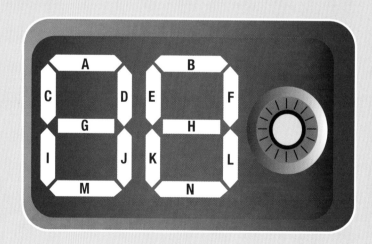

27 DIFFICULTY ✪✪✪✪✪✪✪✪✪  Minute

A game of snooker is in progress. Study this picture for one minute, then see if you can answer the questions on page 28.

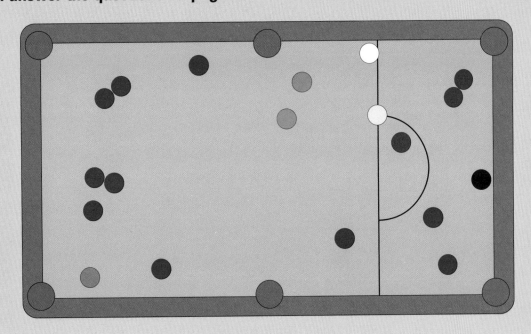

28 DIFFICULTY ✪✪✪✪✪✪✪✪✪ 3 Minutes

is to:

as

is to: a   b   c   d   e

[27] DIFFICULTY ✪✪✪✪✪✪☆☆☆☆

Can you answer these questions about the puzzle on page 27 without looking back?

1. What is the color of the ball closest to the top right pocket?
2. What is the color of the ball closest to the blue ball?
3. What is the color of the ball closest to the brown ball?
4. What is the color of the ball farthest to the right in the picture?
5. How many red balls are on the table?
6. What color is the ball closest to the top center pocket?
7. How many pairs of red balls are touching one another?
8. What color is the ball closest to the bottom left pocket?

29 DIFFICULTY ✪✪✪✪✪✪☆☆☆  3 Minutes

Which number is the odd one out in this collection?

2379 5649

4508 9782

4627 2843

30 DIFFICULTY ✪✪✪✪✪✪✫✫✫✫  **Minutes**

Each block is equal to the sum of the two numbers beneath it.
Find all the missing numbers.

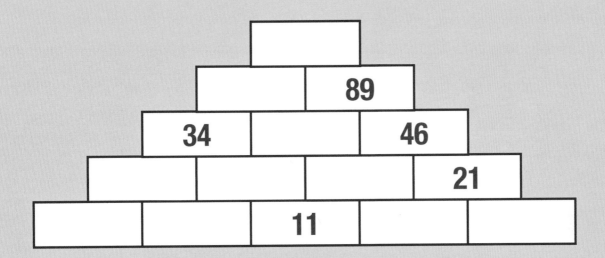

31 DIFFICULTY ✪✪✪✪✪✪✫✫✫✫  **Minutes**

Again, each block is equal to the sum of the two numbers beneath it.
Find all the missing numbers.

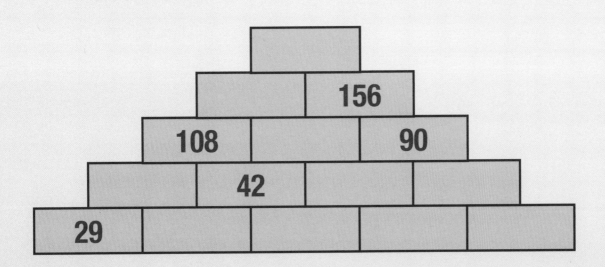

32 DIFFICULTY ★★★★★★★★★★  **Minutes**

Try this number grid. But don't hang around! (See page 25 for advice on how to complete this type of puzzle.)

Top (column) clues:

			5			9												
	4	3	6	8		9	1	9										
	2	1	3	1	9	1	1	2	9	9								
4	1	2	1	5	1	2	1	5	3	3	10		5	5				
4	7	1	1	1	2	3	3	2	1	1	1	4	11	3	4	5	6	10 8 6

Bottom header row:

0 5 9 11 8 1 2 1 1 1 2 2 3 3 4 5 6 15 30 29 14 14 15 16 26 25 13 13 12 11

Left (row) clues:

- 7
- 10
- 13
- 16
- 18
- 20
- 22
- 16 6
- 17 6
- 4 3 5 5
- 3 5 5
- 3 4 4 4 5
- 3 3 3 2 1 5
- 3 2 2 2 1 5
- 3 2 5
- 13 3 5
- 4 1 1 10
- 4 1 1 1 1 12
- 3 1 1 1 1 13
- 2 1 1 14
- 3 1 13
- 2 1 13
- 1 1 13
- 9 13
- 1 4 14
- 1 2 15
- 1 16
- 21
- 20
- 18

33 DIFFICULTY ✪✪✪✪✪✪✪✪✪✪

 **6** Minutes

Every row and column contains the same numbers and signs, but they are arranged in a different order each time. Find the correct order to arrive at the final totals shown.

8	x	7	−	15	+	6	=	47
							=	75
							=	91
							=	71
=		=		=		=		
21		65		79		89		

34 DIFFICULTY ✪✪✪✪✪✪✪✩✩✩  Minutes

Each block is equal to the sum of the two numbers beneath it. Find all the missing numbers.

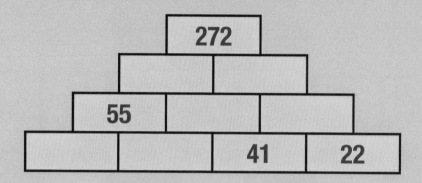

35 DIFFICULTY ✪✪✪✪✪✪✪✩✩✩  Minutes

What number should replace the question mark in this sequence?

71 43 15 86 58 ?

36 DIFFICULTY ✪✪✪✪✪✪✩✩✩✩  Minutes

Make a calculation totaling the figure on the right by inserting the four mathematical signs (+, −, ÷, x) between the numbers shown.

They can be inserted in any order, and one of them has been used twice.

9 3 2 6 4 7 = 9

37 DIFFICULTY ✪✪✪✪✪✪✪✪✪✪

6 Minutes

The value of each shape is the number of sides of each shape multiplied by the number within it. Thus a square containing the number 4 has a value of 16. Can you find a block two squares wide and two squares high with a total value of exactly 100?

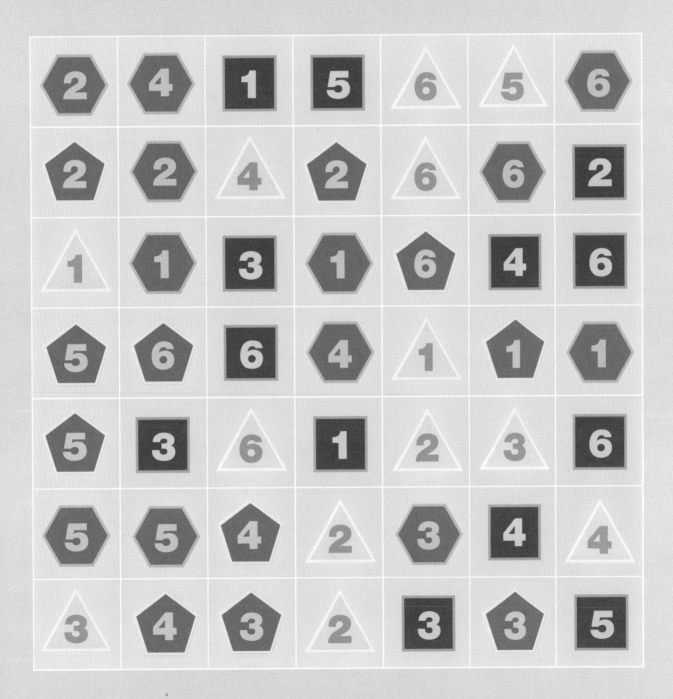

38 DIFFICULTY ✪✪✪✪✪✪✪✪☆☆

Minutes

Make your own way through this number maze. You must pass through all the equals signs.

START

7	x	2
+	3	÷
4	–	5
–	4	+
2	–	8

7	+	5
–	3	x
12	÷	2
+	4	–
6	x	1

=

3	÷	2
x	5	x
4	÷	9
+	6	+
2	+	4

2	x	1
+	7	x
6	+	7
+	8	+
3	–	4

=

÷

10

FINISH

39 DIFFICULTY ✪✪✪✪✪✪✪☆☆☆    15 Minutes

Five cars are driven in five rallies in Europe. Can you name each driver and match him to his vehicle and deduce the rally he won?

	Svensson	Jonsson	Larsson	Magnussen	Hankonen	Spain	Iceland	Italy	Britain	Ireland	Renault	Citroen	Ford	Subaru	Seat	Red	Blue	Orange	Yellow	Black
Gunter																				
Johan																				
Sven																				
Juha																				
Mats																				
Red																
Blue																
Orange																
Yellow																
Black																
Renault										
Citroën										
Ford										
Subaru										
Seat										
Spain					
Iceland					
Italy					
Britain					
Ireland					

1. Svensson didn't win in Iceland, and didn't drive a Ford or a Renault or any blue car.
2. The orange car didn't win in Britain or Spain, and Johan didn't drive it.
3. Sven Magnussen didn't drive a Renault or a Subaru.
4. The Ford that won in Iceland wasn't red.
5. Mats won in Ireland, but not in a Citroën or a Renault.
6. Gunter drove a black car, but he didn't win in Italy, and it wasn't a Seat.
7. Jonsson drove a yellow car, but not in Britain or Ireland, and it wasn't a Renault.
8. Hankonen won in Italy, but it wasn't a Renault.
9. The winning car in Spain was blue, but was not a Citroën.
10. Juha didn't drive a yellow car, and Mats didn't drive an orange one.

 **Minutes**

Using up, down, left, and right only, draw a continuous loop on this grid so that each numbered square contains the correct number of sides bordering it (see examples on the right). You don't need to travel across every dot. We've started the path off for you.

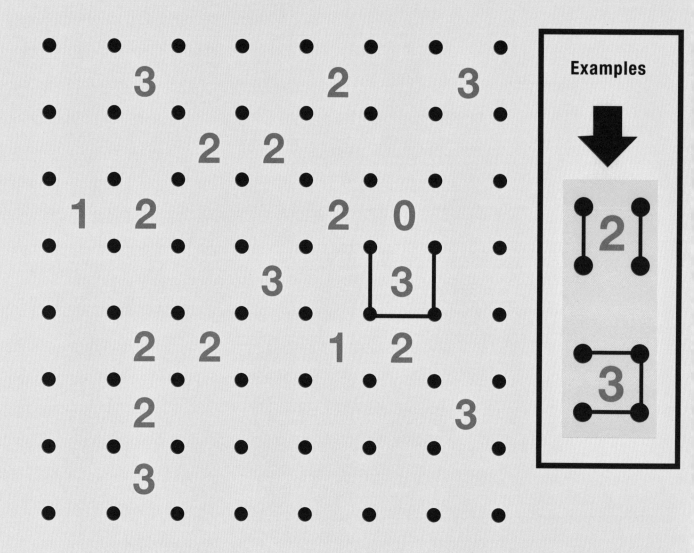

41 DIFFICULTY ✪✪✪✪✪✪✪☆☆☆  **6** Minutes

Each block is equal to the sum of the two numbers beneath it. Find all the missing numbers.

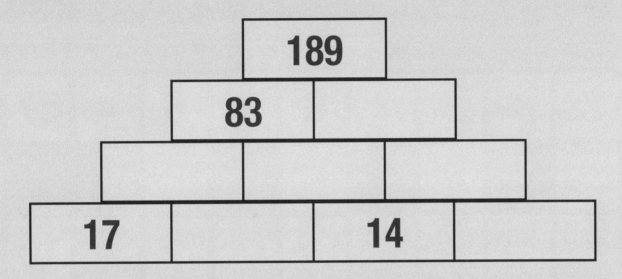

42 DIFFICULTY ✪✪✪✪✪✪☆☆☆☆  **6** Minutes

Can you find a complete set of standard dominoes from 0-0 to 6-6 (28 dominoes in all) by drawing 2 x 1 boxes around this set of numbers?

1	4	2	2	1	3	3	2
3	6	5	5	6	0	0	5
3	5	5	0	3	2	0	0
5	4	1	1	1	4	5	3
5	0	6	1	0	1	6	6
4	6	3	0	6	2	2	2
1	4	3	2	6	4	4	4

43 DIFFICULTY ✪✪✪✪✪✪☆☆☆☆

 **6** Minutes

Every row and column contains the same numbers and signs, but they are arranged in a different order each time. Find the correct order to arrive at the final totals shown.

12	+	9	X	3	−	6	= 57
						=	15
						=	45
						=	81
=		=		=		=	
66		72		33		135	

44 DIFFICULTY ✪✪✪✪✪✪✪✪✪✪  **4** Minutes

Can you put these pieces together to form a 6 x 6 square in which each row, column, and diagonal adds up to the same total?

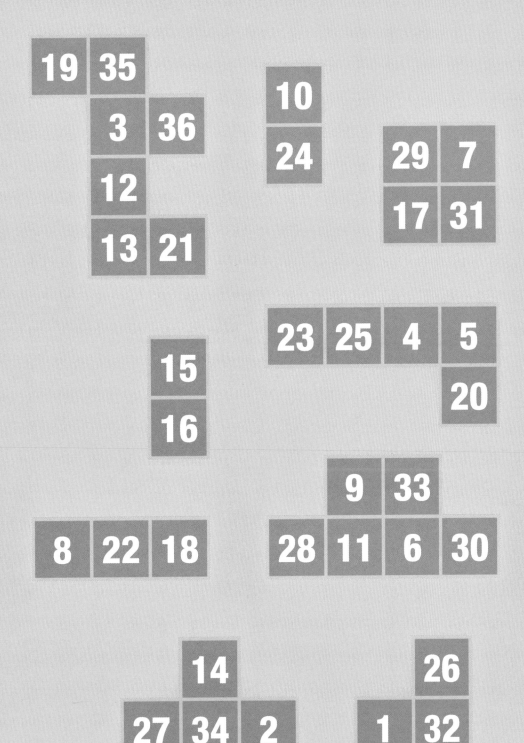

45 DIFFICULTY ✪✪✪✪✪✪✪☆☆☆

 **5** Minutes

Given that scales a and b balance perfectly, how many red balls are needed to balance scale c?

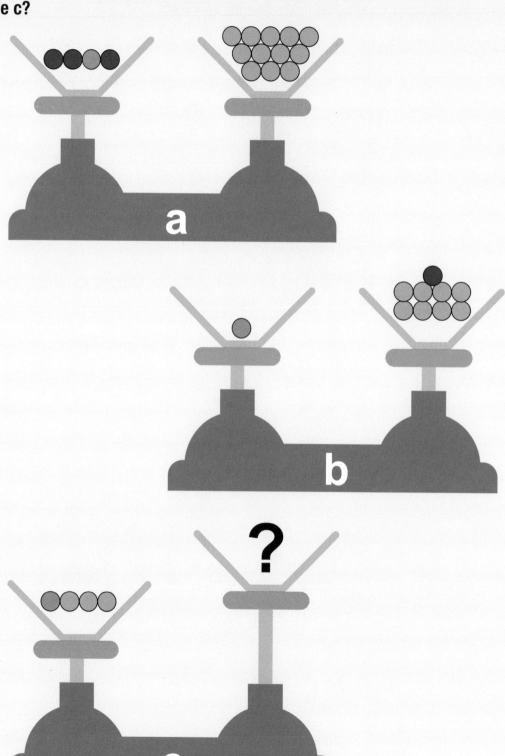

46 DIFFICULTY ✪✪✪✪✪✪✪✪✪  **Minutes**

Which number is the odd one out?

479 891
366 146
255 486

47 DIFFICULTY ✪✪✪✪✪✪✪✪✪  **Minutes**

Which numbers should replace the question marks below?

1 100 24
77 47 54
70 31 ? ?

48 DIFFICULTY ✪✪✪✪✪✪☆☆☆☆  **Minutes**

Make a calculation totaling the figure on the right by inserting the four mathematical signs (+, −, ÷, x) between the numbers shown.

They can be inserted in any order, and one of them has been used twice.

| 7 | | 2 | 4 | 8 | 3 | 5 | = | 5 |

49 DIFFICULTY ✪✪✪✪✪✪☆☆☆☆  **Minutes**

Fill in the grid so that every row, every column, and every 3 x 3 box contains the numbers 1 to 9.

6	8	4		3				
1			6		4			2
5				1			4	3
	4			7	3		9	6
7		2	9					
	9		1		2	8		
					9	7	2	
	3	8				4		9
	1	5	4				6	

50 DIFFICULTY ✩✩✩✩✩✩✩✩✩✩

 6 Minutes

The number 157,643 appears just once in this number-search grid and occurs in a straight line, running either backward or forward in a horizontal, vertical, or diagonal direction. Can you find it?

1	5	7	6	3	4	3	7	6	5	1	1	1
5	5	1	1	6	3	4	7	5	1	5	5	7
4	6	7	5	1	4	1	6	7	6	7	1	5
6	1	1	5	7	6	3	4	1	7	6	5	1
1	5	4	7	1	1	3	5	4	7	1	7	3
4	6	7	5	1	4	1	3	1	5	5	4	6
3	1	7	6	7	5	1	5	7	6	7	1	3
1	6	7	6	4	6	5	6	1	5	6	1	4
4	7	5	1	1	7	4	1	6	1	1	5	5
3	5	5	3	1	3	1	5	5	7	5	7	6
4	1	7	5	3	1	5	7	6	7	4	6	1
1	7	5	4	6	1	5	6	7	6	4	5	5
5	1	5	7	6	3	4	4	3	1	5	3	1

51 DIFFICULTY ✪✪✪✪✪✪✪☆☆☆  **7** Minutes

Can you crack the safe? First decide which of the 14 statements given are false. Then shade out the areas on the combination lock that are labeled with the letters of those false statements (so if you think statement A is false, shade out area A). The remaining lit segments will give you the digital combination required.

Hint: four of the statements are false.

A. Margaret Thatcher was the first female Prime Minister of the UK.
B. Vincent van Gogh died in 1890.
C. UNICEF is the United Nations' charity for children in emergencies.
D. Schiphol Airport is found in Amsterdam.
E. *Star Trek* captain James T. Kirk had the middle name Terrence.
F. In architecture, a campanile is a bell tower.
G. "Somewhere My Love" from *Doctor Zhivago* is also known as "Lara's Theme."
H. There are no even prime numbers.
I. Damascus is the capital city of Syria.
J. A gimlet is a cocktail of gin and lime.
K. The Panama Canal is 5.01 miles long.
L. Taiwan was formerly known as Formosa.
M. Varicella is the medical name for chicken pox.
N. Kahlua is a raspberry-flavored liqueur.

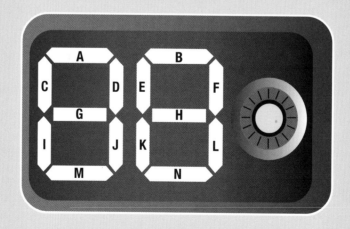

52 DIFFICULTY ✪✪✪☆☆☆☆☆☆☆  6 Minutes

Can you fit these numbers into the grid? One number has already been inserted to help you get started.

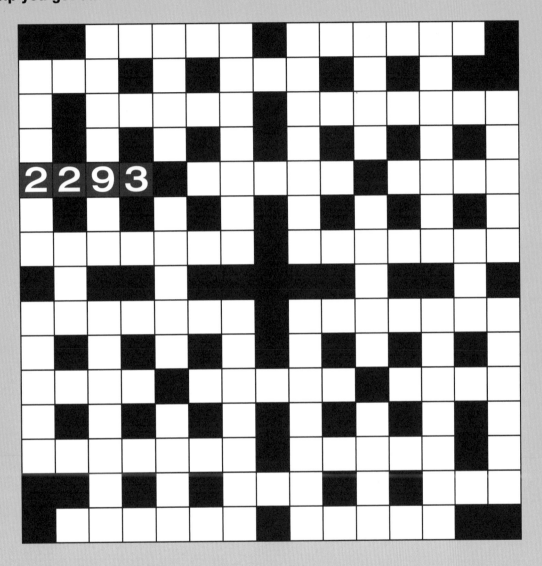

3 Digits	4 Digits	5 Digits	6 Digits	3966343
198	1719	10351	169295	4012952
410	2293	21827	431586	4410723
616	3122	35372	512916	5736533
763	4649	42784	638914	6551484
835	5753	49777		7332976
932	6297	55022	7 Digits	7814903
	7869	67491	1211664	8261243
	8434	71864	1814762	9123453
		74713	2313394	9529125
		85493	3132654	

53 DIFFICULTY ✪✪✪✪✪✪✪✪☆☆  **3** Minutes

Which set of numbers is the odd one out?

2	7
3	8

a

8	1
9	2

b

4	9
1	6

c

8	3
7	2

d

54 DIFFICULTY ✪✪✪✪☆✪☆☆✪☆  **3** Minutes

What numbers should replace the question marks in the following sequence?

7	15
2	6

a

6	11
5	13

b

5	7
8	20

c

?	?
?	?

d

55 DIFFICULTY ✪✪✪✪✪✪✪✪✪✪  3 Minutes

What number should replace the question mark in the following sequence?

39974   47893   39774   47693   ?

56 DIFFICULTY ✪✪✪✪✪✪✪✪✪✪ 4 Minutes

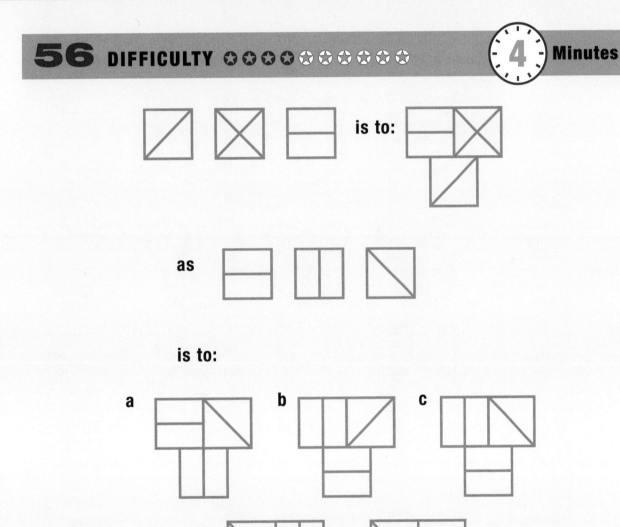

These animals each represent a number between 1 and 5. If a dog is worth 5, can you figure out the correct values of the other animals in order to make a successful sum?

58 DIFFICULTY ✪✪✪✪✪✪✪✪✪✪  Minutes

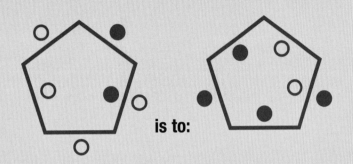

is to:

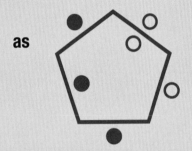

as

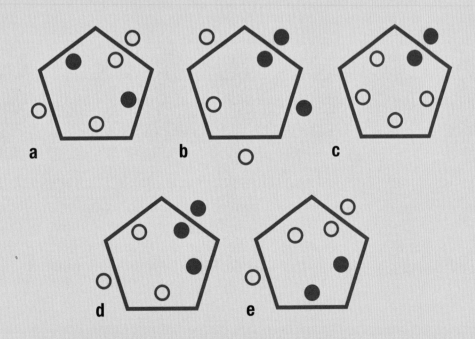

is to:

a   b   c

d   e

59 DIFFICULTY ✪✪✪✪✪✪☆☆☆☆  **6** Minutes

What number should replace the question mark in the pie below?

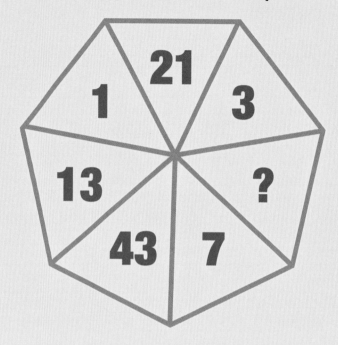

60 DIFFICULTY ✪✪✪✪✪✪✪✪☆☆  **6** Minutes

Each block is equal to the sum of the numbers beneath it. Note that the upper blocks lie on 1, 2, or 3 other blocks. Find all the missing numbers.

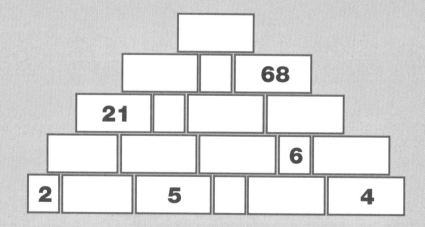

61 DIFFICULTY ✪✪✪✪✪✪✩✩✩✩

5 Minutes

Each block is equal to the sum of the two numbers beneath it.
Find all the missing numbers.

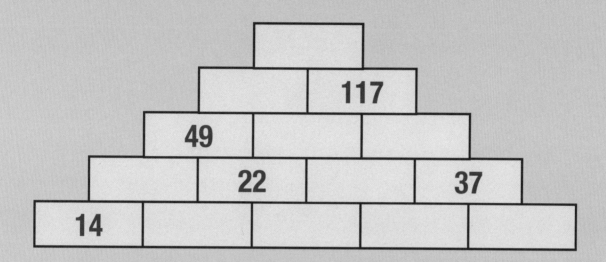

62 DIFFICULTY ✪✪✪✪✩✩✩✩✩✩

3 Minutes

Which set of numbers is the odd one out?

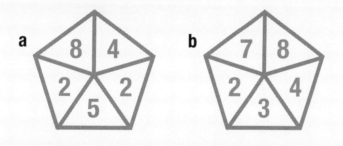

63 DIFFICULTY ✪✪✪✪✪✪✪✪✩✩  **Minutes**

By drawing three straight lines, can you divide this circle into five sections, each containing five wedges in different colors? The lines run from edge to edge of the circle and can be drawn without taking pencil from paper!

64 DIFFICULTY ✪✪✪✪✪✪✪✪✪✪  Minutes

The three bubbles on top of each hexagon contain numbers that, when added together and subtracted from the sum of the three balls below the hexagon, equal the number inside the hexagon. Fill in all the missing numbers.

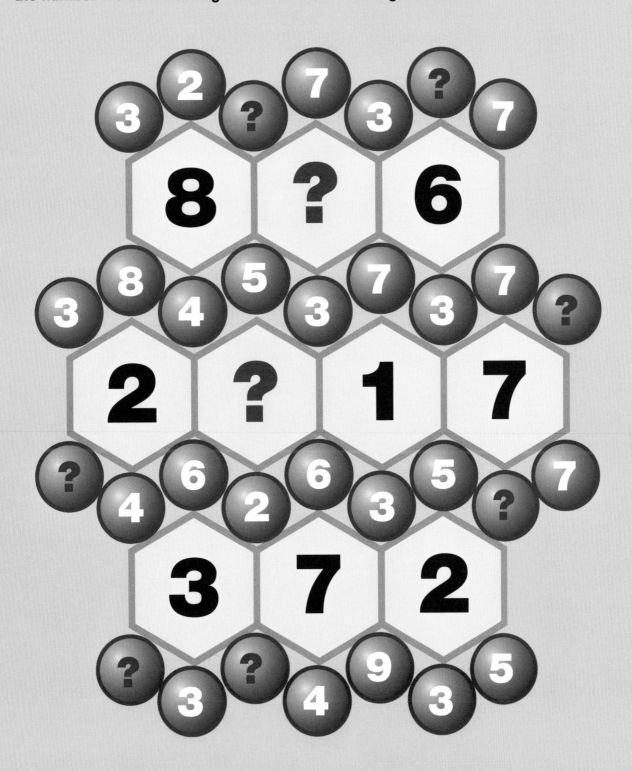

65 DIFFICULTY ✪✪✪✪✪✪✪☆☆  10 Minutes

Travel from the cue ball to the black 8 ball with a successful sum that begins with, and totals, 8.

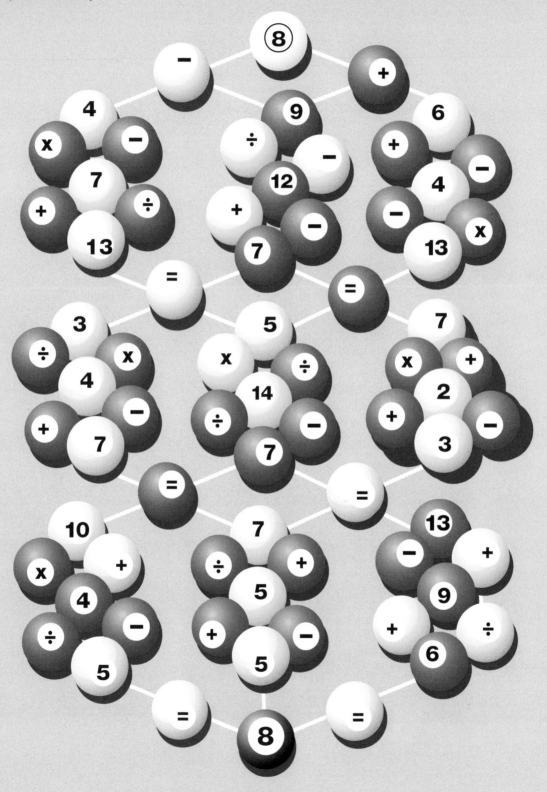

66 DIFFICULTY ✪✪✪✪✪✪✪✪✪  6 Minutes

Each row and column contains the same numbers and signs, but they are arranged in a different order each time. Find the correct order to arrive at the final totals shown.

5	+	9	x	2	–	7	=	21
							=	50
							=	22
							=	40
=		=		=		=		
42		70		48		36		

67 DIFFICULTY ✪✪✪✩✩✩✩✩✩✩  **2** Minutes

Each block is equal to the sum of the two numbers beneath it. Find all the missing numbers.

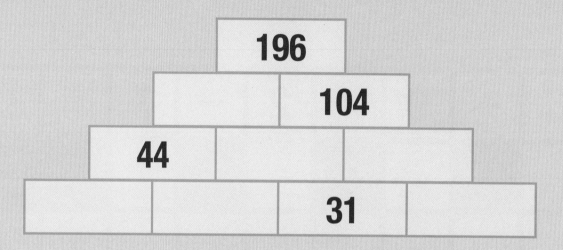

68 DIFFICULTY ✪✪✪✪✪✪✪✩✩✪  **6** Minutes

What three-digit number should replace the question mark in the following sequence?

952 738

619 527

386 ?

69 DIFFICULTY ✪✪✪✪✪✪✪✪✪✪  **Minutes**

Which number is the odd one out?

82496   61872

41648   72184

51560

70 DIFFICULTY ✪✪✪✪✪✪✪✪✪✪  **Minutes**

Make a calculation totaling the figure on the right by inserting the four mathematical signs (+, −, ÷, x) between the numbers shown.

They can be inserted in any order, and one of them has been used twice.

| 52 | | 27 | | 34 | | 9 | | 19 | | 66 | = | 161 |

71 DIFFICULTY ✪✩✩✩✩✩✩✩✩ 6 Minutes

Can you fit these numbers into the grid? One number has already been inserted to help you get started.

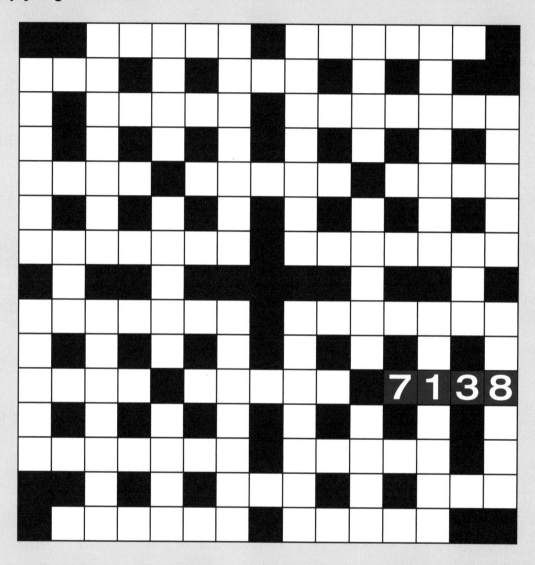

3 Digits	4 Digits	5 Digits	78664	7 Digits	5365044
234	1871	10332	95392	1238269	6929644
302	2630	35760		1248085	7013523
412	3673	40001	6 Digits	2474734	7867656
430	3678	49031	335148	2869824	9818724
608	3690	57356	588994	3056462	9865325
612	5521	64510	632915	3414421	
	~~7138~~	65287	732868	4676623	
	9266	74542		5244448	

72 DIFFICULTY ✪✪✪✪✪✪✪✪✪✪  **6** Minutes

Which of the four boxed figures (a, b, c, or d) completes the set?

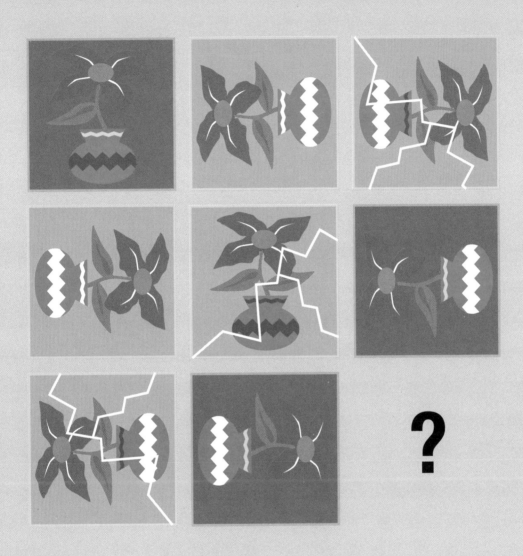

a   b   c   d

73 DIFFICULTY ✪✪✪✪✪✪✪☆☆☆

 **6** Minutes

Each block is equal to the sum of the two numbers beneath it.
Find all the missing numbers.

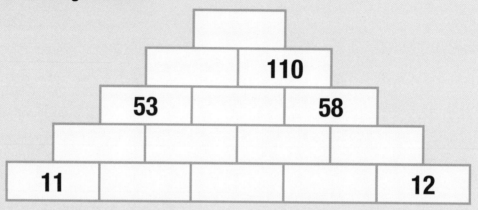

74 DIFFICULTY ✪✪✪✪✪✪☆☆☆☆

 **5** Minutes

The value of each shape is the number of sides of each shape, multiplied by the number within it. Thus, a square containing the number 4 has a value of 16.

Find a block two squares wide and two squares high with a total value of exactly 100.

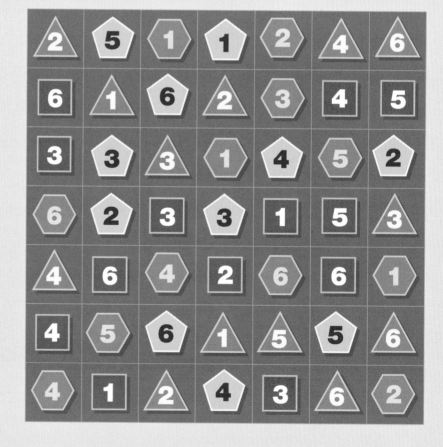

75 DIFFICULTY ✪✪✪✪✪✪✪☆☆☆  2 Minutes

Study this picture for two minutes, then see if you can answer the questions on page 62.

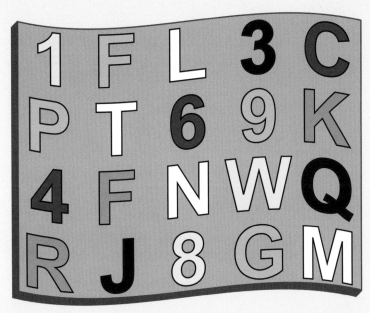

76 DIFFICULTY ✪✪✪✪✪✪☆☆☆☆ 6 Minutes

Which number should be in the empty triangle?

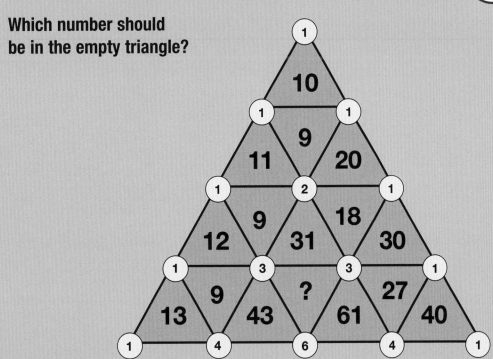

[75] DIFFICULTY ✪✪✪✪✪✪✪✪✪✪

Can you answer these questions about the puzzle on page 61 without looking back?

1. Which letter appears twice?

2. Which color is used for more letters than any other color?

3. Which letter or number is to the right of the N?

4. Which is the only red letter?

5. Which letter or number is directly above the R?

6. Adding together all of the numbers produces what total?

7. Which letter or number is directly between K and M?

8. How many letters are there in total?

77 DIFFICULTY ✪✪✪✪✪✪✪✪✪✪ 5 Minutes

Make a calculation totaling the figure on the right by inserting the four mathematical signs (+, −, ÷, x) between the numbers shown.

They can be inserted in any order, and one of them has been used twice.

39 **13** **64** **47** **59** **12** = **17**

78 DIFFICULTY ✪✪✪✪✪✪✪✪✪✪  6 Minutes

The number 234,567 appears just once in this number-search grid and occurs in a straight line, running either backward or forward in a horizontal, vertical, or diagonal direction. Can you find it?

2	3	2	7	7	2	7	2	5	4	3	2
7	3	4	2	3	4	6	5	7	3	3	7
2	7	2	4	2	5	6	7	2	4	4	2
2	3	5	5	3	3	6	5	5	7	3	7
2	5	2	4	4	4	4	7	4	4	3	6
7	3	7	5	3	3	2	5	5	3	2	5
6	5	6	2	2	2	3	7	6	4	2	4
5	7	3	2	3	3	6	3	6	3	6	3
3	2	5	5	3	4	2	5	5	2	5	2
4	5	4	4	5	6	5	4	4	4	4	2
2	3	7	5	3	7	3	6	2	3	3	7
2	3	4	5	6	2	7	3	2	7	2	2

79 DIFFICULTY ✪✪✪✪✪✪☆☆☆☆ ⏱ **5** Minutes

The number 837,436,951 appears just once in this number-search grid and occurs in a straight line, running either backward or forward in a horizontal, vertical, or diagonal direction. Can you find it?

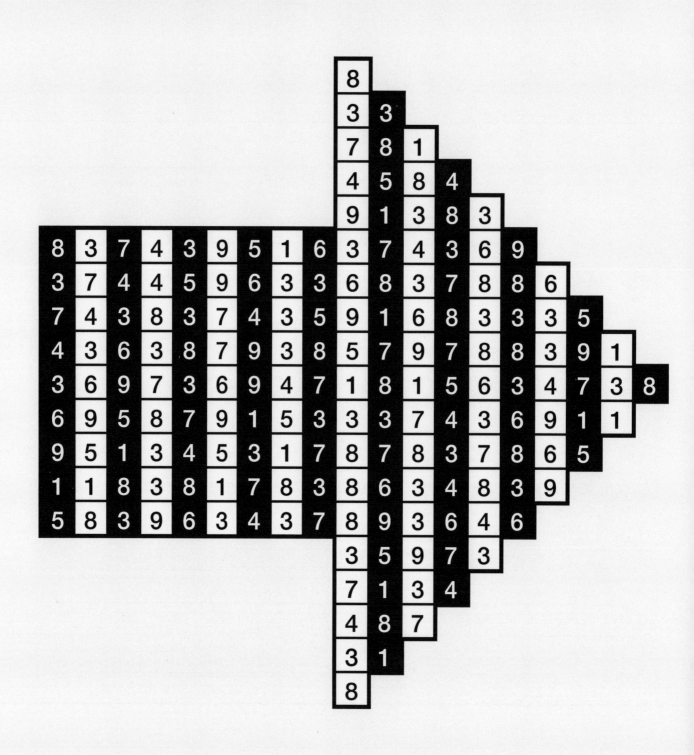

80 DIFFICULTY ✪✪✪✪✪✪✪☆☆  Minutes

     is to:

as

is to:

   a   b   c   d   e

81 DIFFICULTY ✪✪✪✪✪✪✪✪☆☆  Minutes

Fill in the grid so that every row, every column, and every 3 x 3 box contains the numbers 1 to 9.

	6	4				1		
5				2	1		6	3
1				6				9
			8		7	3	1	
	4	9				7		6
	3		6		5		9	
6			5	7				2
	8		2		9		7	
	7	2		8		4		

The three bubbles on top of each hexagon contain numbers that, when added together and subtracted from the sum of the three balls below the hexagon, equal the number inside the hexagon. Fill in all the missing numbers.

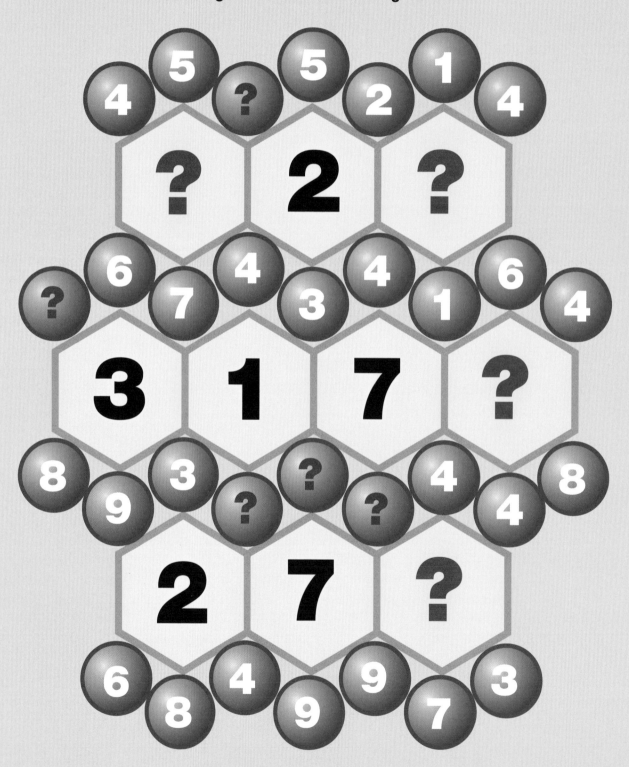

83 DIFFICULTY ★★★☆☆☆☆☆☆☆  6 Minutes

Can you fit these numbers into the grid? One number has already been inserted to help you get started.

3 Digits	4 Digits	5 Digits	96124	7 Digits	6132757
154	1392	24021	97867	1731619	7493013
409	3409	32890		2059640	7874462
417	3825	50473	6 Digits	2404365	8577246
632	4592	57829	104631	4129296	8750242
694	6148	61166	576470	4376623	9678439
787	6304	75909	682537	5461238	
	6439	76916	921565	5591772	
	9785	82146		6072813	

84 DIFFICULTY ✪✪✪✪✪✪✪✪✩✩  **Minutes**

Can you crack the safe? First decide which of the fourteen statements given are false. Then shade out the areas on the combination lock that are labeled with the letters of those false statements (so if you think statement A is false, shade out area A). The remaining lit segments will give you the digital combination required.

Hint: five of the statements are false.

A.   The dog Laika went into space in 1957.
B.   On the stock market, a bull buys new share issues hoping to make a profit.
C.   The American War of 1812 began in 1815.
D.   We are currently living in the Cenozoic era.
E.   The flag of Germany is black, red, and gold.
F.   The Bauhaus art movement was founded in 1919.
G.   In 1971, George C. Scott refused an Oscar for his leading role in *Patton*.
H.   The term *blitzkrieg* means "lightning war."
I.   Testa Rossa is a famous model of Lotus car.
J.   In the NATO alphabet, the letter Q is signified by Quebec.
K.   Pathophobia is the fear of mazes.
L.   A collection of penguins can be called a rookery.
M.   James Fenimore Cooper wrote *The Last of the Mohicans*.
N.   Charles Dickens wrote under the pen name of Box.

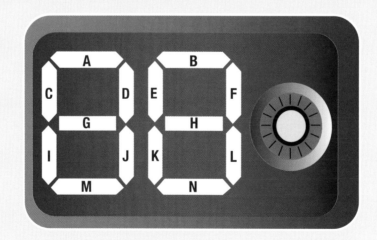

85 DIFFICULTY ✪✪✪✪✪✪✪✪✪✪

Make a calculation totaling the figure on the right by inserting the four mathematical signs (+, −, ÷, x) between the numbers shown.

They can be inserted in any order, and one of them has been used twice.

| 31 | | 17 | | 15 | | 3 | | 9 | | 42 | = | 53 |

86 DIFFICULTY ✪✪✪✪✪✪✪✪✪✪

The animals each represent a number between 1 and 6. If a mouse is worth 2, can you figure out the correct values of the other animals in order to make a successful sum?

87 DIFFICULTY ✪✪✪✪✪✪☆☆☆☆  3 Minutes

What number should replace the question mark?

376829
18144
?   16   6

88 DIFFICULTY ✪✪✪✪✪✪☆☆☆☆  5 Minutes

7	10	14	19
6		13	18
	7		16
1		8	13

Which of the cross-shaped sections (a, b, c, or d) is the missing section in the grid?

```
     8              9              9              9
  5     11       4     11       4     12       5     12
     5              4              5              4

     a              b              c              d
```

89 DIFFICULTY ✪✪✪✪✪✪✪✪✪ ⏱ 5 Minutes

Each block is equal to the sum of the two numbers beneath it.
Can you find all the missing numbers?

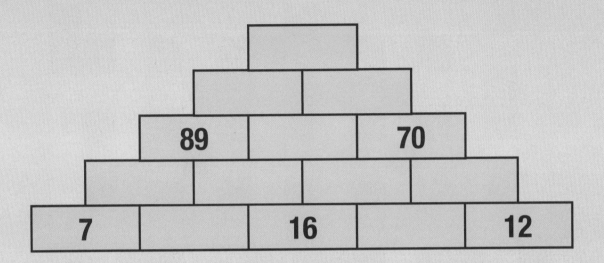

90 DIFFICULTY ✪✪✪✪✪✪✪✪✪ ⏱ 6 Minutes

Again, each block is equal to the sum of the two numbers beneath it.
Can you find all the missing numbers?

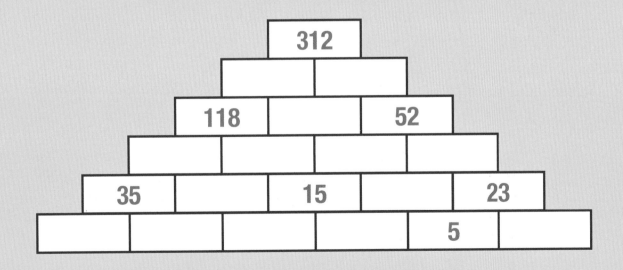

91 DIFFICULTY ✪✪✪✪✪✪✪✪✪  Minutes

Can you fit these numbers into the grid? One number has already been inserted to help you get started.

3 Digits	4 Digits	5 Digits	75959	7 Digits	5774287
212	4620	27401	87283	1014682	7567176
228	4747	28774		1936204	7877068
805	4805	28905	6 Digits	2233017	8421185
864	5075	31778	251515	2379137	8919294
914	5303	34053	258045	3326884	9210392
~~937~~	5353	41875	845213	4287342	
	9278	42813	867394	4878372	
	9965	72097		5273874	

92 DIFFICULTY ✪✪✪✪✪✪✪✪✪✪  6 Minutes

Can you draw 2 x 1 boxes around this set of numbers to give a set of every possible domino from 0–0 to 4–4; i.e., fifteen dominoes in all?

0	4	2	1	4	1
2	3	2	4	1	1
1	2	0	2	3	3
2	4	3	0	1	0
4	4	3	3	0	0

93 DIFFICULTY ✪✪✪✪✪✪✪✪✪✪  2 Minutes

Each block is equal to the sum of the two numbers beneath it. Can you find all the missing numbers?

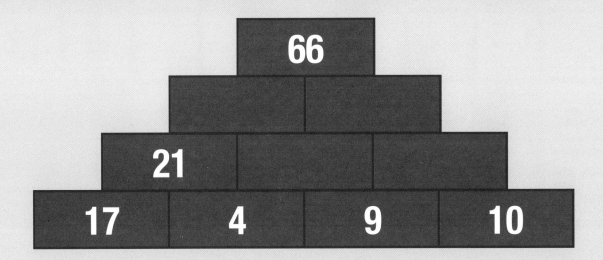

94 DIFFICULTY ●●●●☆☆☆☆☆☆

6 Minutes

Each row and column contains the same numbers and signs, but they are arranged in a different order each time. Find the correct order to arrive at the final totals shown.

13	x	2	–	6	+	9	=	29
							=	41
							=	23
							=	43
=		=		=		=		
36		16		85		53		

95 DIFFICULTY  5 Minutes

Make a calculation totaling the figure on the right by inserting the four mathematical signs (+, −, ÷, x) between the numbers shown.

They can be inserted in any order, and one of them has been used twice.

| 16 | | 4 | | 20 | | 6 | | 37 | | 8 | = | 43 |

96 DIFFICULTY  3 Minutes

Which number is the odd one out?

7121114   1438

8131215   38710

6111013   2769

97 DIFFICULTY ✪✪✪✪✪✪✪☆☆☆ ④ Minutes

The number 35,174 appears just once in this grid and occurs in a straight line, running either backward or forward in a horizontal, vertical, or diagonal direction; however, as you can see, the numbers are backward! Can you locate it?

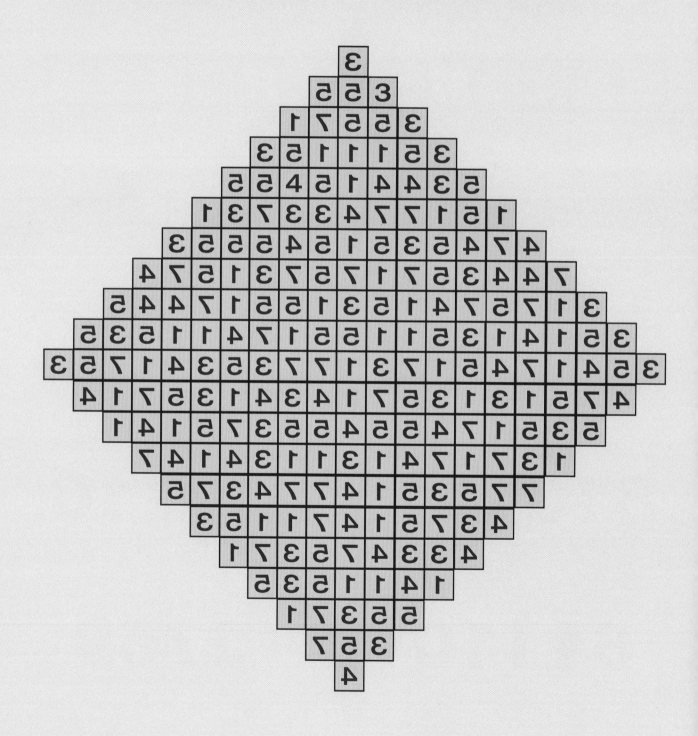

98 DIFFICULTY ✪✪✪✪✪✪✪✩✩✪

You'll go crackers when you've completed this number grid. See page 25 for instructions on how to complete this type of puzzle.

Column clues (top):

```
                                      5
                              5  1        1     1 1
        1 2 4 6        6 2 1 5      7 5 4 2 2 2 2 3 3
        7 5 3 1 7 8 8 1 1 2 1 7 4 4 3 3 3 3 3 3 3 6 6 5 4 3
  5 7 9 7 1 2 4 5 6 4 6 8 9 2 3 2 2 4 6 8 9 10 11 10 10 9 9 8 8 7
```

Row clues (left):

```
                7
               12
               12
               17
               13
          2  5  6
       4  3  1  6
  6  2  2  3  2
     8  1  1  2
        7  2  2
        6  1  1
        5  2  2
        3  4  1
        2  6  2
        1  6  2
        5  3  3
           1  8
           1 10
        1  3  6
     1  3  1  4
     1  3  4  2
           7  7
           7 10
  2  1  1 11
           2 12
           2 12
           2 13
           2 13
           2 14
           2 14
```

99 DIFFICULTY ✪✪✪✪✪✪✪✪✪✪  4 Minutes

By drawing three straight lines, can you divide this flower into five sections, each containing six differently colored flowers?

100 DIFFICULTY ✪✪✪✪✪✪✪✪✪✪  7 Minutes

Can you crack the safe? First decide which of the fourteen statements given are false. Then shade out the areas on the combination lock that are labeled with the letters of those false statements (so if you think statement A is false, shade out area A). The remaining lit segments will give you the digital combination required.

Hint: three of the statements are false.

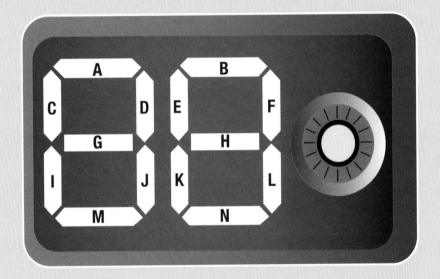

A. The ladies' version of golf's Ryder Cup contest is played for the Curtis Cup.
B. Your phalanges are found in your hands and feet.
C. The unit of frequency is called the avis.
D. Shakespeare's line "A plague o' both your houses" comes from *Romeo and Juliet*.
E. Delta is the fourth letter of the Greek alphabet.
F. Yale University is in the state of Connecticut.
G. Spiders, millipedes, and centipedes are all types of arachnids.
H. Methuselah was the apostle who replaced Judas.
I. Hera was the mythological Greek queen of the gods.
J. Jupiter is the farthest planet in the solar system.
K. St. Francis of Assisi is the patron saint of Italy.
L. Rocinante was the horse of Don Quixote.
M. On a suit of armor, the gorget protects the neck.
N. Matthew is the first book of the Bible's New Testament.

101 DIFFICULTY ✪✩✩✪✩✪✩✩✩✩  Minutes

The final hands in five poker tournaments are described here.
Who won which, with which hands, and what were their nicknames?

1. Steve Stone won in Paris, not with a royal flush.
2. "Animal" Lopez won with a full house.
3. The "Tornado" won the Vegas Open, not with three kings or ace high.
4. Simon won with two pairs, not in London or Reno.
5. Barry "Top Hat" didn't win in Monte Carlo.
6. Julie Kelly didn't win in Vegas or with a royal flush.
7. Reno was won with three kings, not by "Raiser."
8. Jackson didn't win in Vegas.

	Kelly	Jackson	Lopez	Stone	Foster	Full house	Royal flush	Two pairs	Three kings	Ace high	Vegas Open	London Classic	Reno Masters	Paris Match	Monte Carlo Grand Prix	Tornado	Riches	Animal	Raiser	Top Hat
Dave																				
Steve																				
Julie																				
Barry																				
Simon																				
Tornado																					
Riches																					
Animal																					
Raiser																					
Top Hat																					
Vegas Open																					
London Classic																					
Reno Masters																					
Paris Match																					
Monte Carlo Grand Prix																					
Full house																					
Royal flush																					
Two pairs																					
Three kings																					
Ace high																					

102 DIFFICULTY ✪✪✪✪✪✪✪✪✩✩✩  **Minutes**

Given that scales A and B balance perfectly, how many bananas are needed to balance scale C?

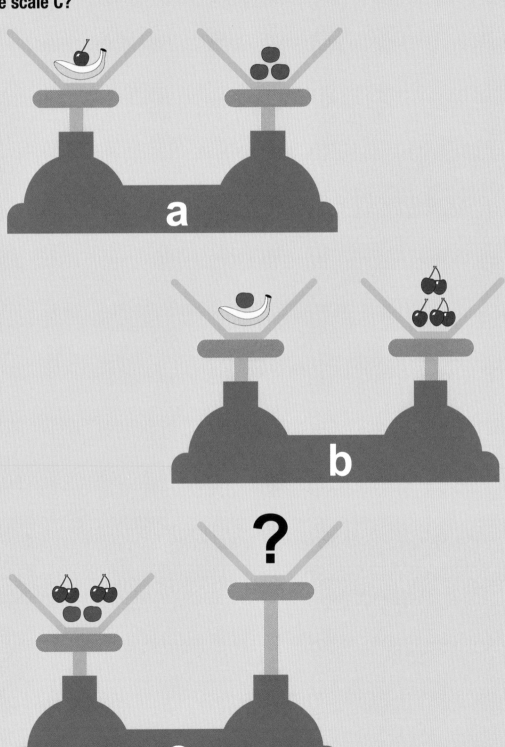

103 DIFFICULTY ✪✪✪✪✪✪✪☆☆☆  Minutes

Move from any platform on the bottom level to any platform on the top level using only ladders and moving only up. Black numbers must be added to your running total, red numbers subtracted. At no point can your running total go below 0.

104 DIFFICULTY ✪✪✪✪✪✪✪✪✪✪

 **6 Minutes**

Can you fit these numbers into the grid? One number has already been inserted to help you get started.

3 Digits	4 Digits	5 Digits	91626	7 Digits	4513243
621	3205	13492	95712	1351092	7295876
645	3935	13552		1791541	7315112
731	5543	14178	6 Digits	2391951	7364723
753	5792	21826	285826	2400930	9345091
961	8178	25162	312781	3648176	9720606
~~972~~	8942	26393	615772	3754062	
	9542	40939	910393	4050730	
	9767	42564		4118024	

105 DIFFICULTY ✪✪✪✪✪✩✩✩✩✩  Minutes

Make a calculation totaling the figure on the right by inserting the four mathematical signs (+, −, ÷, x) between the numbers shown.

They can be inserted in any order, and one of them has been used twice.

| 24 | | 6 | | 9 | | 14 | | 11 | | 2 | = | 78 |

106 DIFFICULTY ✪✪✪✪✪✩✩✩✩✩  Minutes

Again, make another calculation totaling the figure on the right by inserting the four mathematical signs (+, −, ÷, x) between the numbers shown.

They can be inserted in any order, and one of them has been used twice.

| 11 | | 4 | | 12 | | 6 | | 7 | | 10 | = | 31 |

107 DIFFICULTY ✪✪✪✪✪✪✪✪✪✪

 2 Minutes

What numbers should replace the question marks?

1	8	9	4	?
10	5	6	13	?

108 DIFFICULTY ✪✪✪✪✪✪✪✪✪✪

 10 Minutes

Fill in the grid so that every row, every column, and every 3 x 3 box contains the numbers 1 to 9.

2			7			6		
	4		8					3
			2		4		5	1
	7	3						2
6					2		3	
		8		1			7	
4						3		
		6		4	8			7
	8	7	3				6	

Which of the four boxed figures (a, b, c, or d) completes the set?

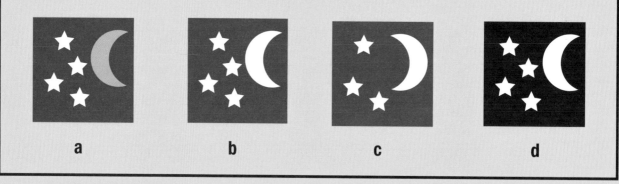

110 DIFFICULTY ✪✪✪✩✩✩✩✩✩✩  6 Minutes

Can you fit these numbers into the grid? One number has already been inserted to help you get started.

3 Digits	4 Digits	5 Digits	86920	7 Digits	6283767
~~283~~	2484	21388	87027	3205425	6319083
286	2682	25614		3380514	7042926
410	3170	35243	**6 Digits**	3714268	7391274
462	3568	39520	404125	4472925	8120680
871	5243	50416	426398	4743203	8271975
875	5902	57327	731935	4868913	
	9209	62524	765382	5341273	
	9679	69593		5746480	

111 DIFFICULTY ✪✪✪✪✪✪✪✪✪✪  **Minutes**

The value of each shape is the number of sides on the shape, multiplied by the number within it. Thus, a square containing the number 4 has a value of 16. Can you find a block two squares wide and two squares high with a total value of exactly 50?

112 DIFFICULTY ✪✪✪✪✪✪✪✪✪✪  **3** Minutes

Make a calculation totaling the figure on the right by inserting the four mathematical signs (+, −, ÷, x) between the numbers shown.

They can be inserted in any order, and one of them has been used twice.

46		13		94		36		39		4	=	212

113 DIFFICULTY ✪✪✪✪✪✪✪✪✪✪  **10** Minutes

Five children visit five stores to buy candies in varying quantities. Can you match each child to the store, and the amount and kind of candies they bought?

	Billy	Amy	Danny	Milly	Titch	Bag	Pound	Handful	5	2	Toffee	Aniseed balls	Licorice	Lemon drops	Chocolate whirl
Watson's															
The Cabin															
Supermarket															
Tuck Shop															
Candyland															
Toffee															
Aniseed balls															
Licorice															
Lemon drops															
Chocolate whirl															
Bag															
Pound															
Handful															
5															
2															

1. Billy bought a handful of lemon drops, not at the supermarket.
2. You can't buy just two toffees anywhere, and Danny and Amy didn't get those.
3. Titch got aniseed balls from the Tuck Shop.
4. Only Candyland sells toffee, but not by the bag or the handful.
5. You can't buy two of anything at the supermarket. Amy didn't go there.
6. Watson's is the only place that sells by the pound, but they don't sell chocolate whirls.

114 DIFFICULTY ✪✪✪✪✪✪✪☆☆☆

 10 Minutes

Move from the top red square to the bottom red square, creating a series of sums. You must pass through an equals sign every fourth square. You may move to any adjacent square, but may not move diagonally.

8

	−	6	=	2	=	6	−	3
=	7			+	4			=
1	+			5	=	7	+	3
	4	=		−				X
		5	X	3	=	15		4
=	2	+				÷	5	=
7			=	2			=	12
÷	4	−	6	÷	9	+	3	÷
7	=	1		12	=		=	2
	2	−				X	6	
	X	3	=	6	+	2	=	

8

115 DIFFICULTY ✪✪✪✪✪☆☆☆☆☆  4 Minutes

The number 123,456 appears three times in this grid and always in straight lines, running either backward or forward in a horizontal, vertical, or diagonal direction. Can you locate all three occurences?

1	2	3	4	5	1	2	3	4	5	6	1	5	1	5
3	2	1	4	6	5	4	3	2	5	5	4	2	6	5
2	5	3	2	1	4	4	5	4	4	3	3	2	5	1
4	1	5	4	3	3	5	1	4	2	4	1	1	2	5
5	4	2	1	5	2	2	6	1	5	1	5	3	2	6
6	3	4	3	3	1	6	3	4	2	5	4	6	1	4
1	5	2	2	1	6	2	3	4	4	6	1	2	1	3
6	2	4	1	5	2	2	3	6	5	4	3	3	1	1
4	1	3	4	1	1	3	1	4	6	6	2	3	2	1
5	3	3	3	4	6	5	4	2	5	1	4	2	3	2
6	2	3	1	5	2	3	2	5	4	5	5	1	4	3
1	2	1	3	2	2	1	3	2	3	4	6	6	6	5
1	1	4	2	1	4	2	4	5	2	2	3	4	5	4
3	2	1	5	2	1	5	6	3	1	6	1	2	5	5
1	3	4	5	6	1	5	6	2	3	4	5	6	1	6

116 DIFFICULTY ✪✪✪✪✪✪✩✩✩  6 Minutes

Each row and column contains the same numbers and signs, but they are arranged in a different order each time. Find the correct order to arrive at the final totals shown.

31	+	16	x	12	−	23	=	541
						=	207
						=	387
						=	320
=		=		=		=	
456		123		200		632	

117 DIFFICULTY ✪✪✪✪✪✪✩✩✩✩ ⏱ **5** Minutes

Fill in the grid so that every row, every column, and every 3 x 3 box contains the numbers 1 to 9.

9		3						
			3	5	6		9	
6				9		1		3
	4		2				3	6
	2	7			1			
	5			4		7		
		1			8			9
	3		7					1
			2	6			3	8

118 DIFFICULTY ✪✪✪✪✪✩✩✩✩✩ ⏱ **4** Minutes

PEF is to: ACE

as EBA

is to: **a** CAP   **b** 608

c FOE   **d** COP   **e** 669

119 DIFFICULTY ✪✪✪✪✪✪✪✪✪✪  **5** Minutes

Which of the four boxed figures (a, b, c, or d) completes the set?

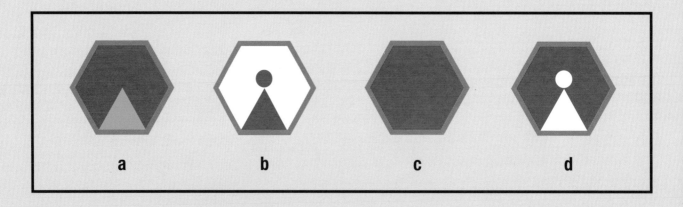

a b c d

120 DIFFICULTY ✪✪✪✪✪✪✪✪✪✪  **30** Minutes

Will you be able to charge through this number grid in record time? If you need any help completing this puzzle, refer to the instructions on page 25.

Column clues (top):

Row 1: 6 12 ... 5 ... 2 2 8 4
Row 2: 5 7 10 ... 7 2 3 16 14 11 ... 4 8 15 ... 2 1 12 12 9 4 6
Row 3: 1 3 6 18 17 16 14 2 2 3 4 4 4 15 15 17 7 7 22 18 19 14 12 1 3 5 7 10 23 24

Row clues (left):

				0
				1
	1	3	1	
	1	3	2	
2	4	1	1	
3	3	1	2	
3	3	3	2	1
3	1	5	2	2
3	2	4	2	2
4	2	5	1	3
4	3	7	2	3
4	3	7	2	3
	5	4	12	3
		6	17	3
			24	3
			24	2
			24	2
		13	9	2
		14	9	2
		7	16	3
		6	16	3
		7	16	4
			23	5
		10	10	6
		4	9	7
		3	11	6
		1	8	5
			5	4
			2	3
				2

121 DIFFICULTY ✪✪✪✪✪✪✪☆☆☆  5 Minutes

The number 516,783,962,014 appears just once in this grid and occurs in a triangular shape, running in either a clockwise or counterclockwise direction but not starting in any particular square, similar to the example shown here:

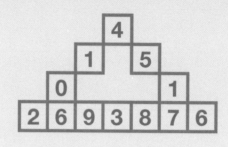

Can you locate it?

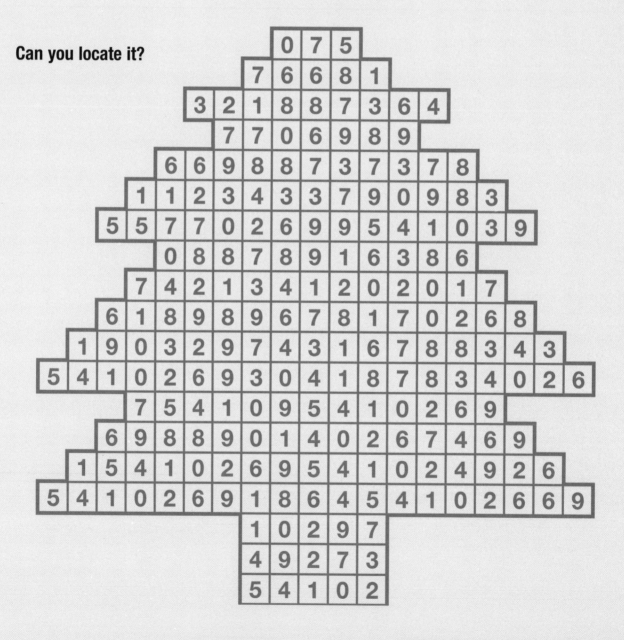

122 DIFFICULTY ✪✪✪✪✪✪✩✩✩  Minutes

Can you join the images in a logical order? Your lines may cross but you may not follow the same path twice.

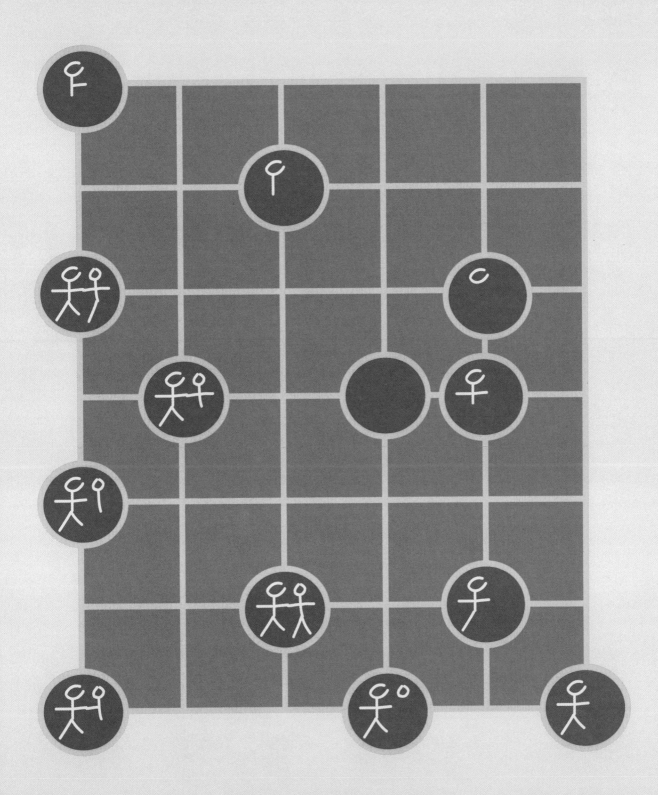

123 DIFFICULTY ✪✪✪✪✪✪☆☆☆☆

Make a calculation totaling the figure on the right by inserting the four mathematical signs (+, −, ÷, x) between the numbers shown.

They can be inserted in any order, and one of them has been used twice.

| 53 | | 23 | | 16 | | 66 | | 18 | | 87 | = | 110 |

124 DIFFICULTY ✪✪✪✪✪✪✪☆☆☆

The three bubbles on top of each hexagon contain numbers that, when added together and subtracted from the sum of the three balls below the hexagon, equal the number inside the hexagon. Fill in all the missing numbers.

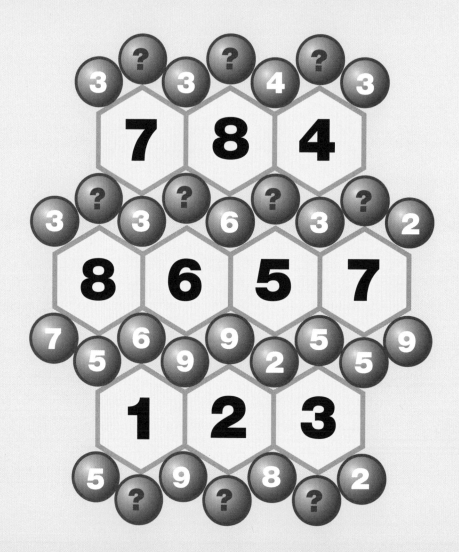

125 DIFFICULTY ✪✪✪✪✪✪✪✪✩✩

 **4** Minutes

Which numbers should replace the question marks in the bottom circles?

6 21 2

3 21 4

6 84 8

? ? ?

126 DIFFICULTY ✪✪✪✪✪✪✪✪✩✩

10 Minutes

Five ladies are off on mind-expanding vacations with a travel partner. Can you figure out who goes where, with whom, and for what sort of vacation?

	Brenda	Maureen	Dierdre	Louise	Nora	Daughter	Husband	Sister	Neighbor	Mom	Spa	Health farm	Yoga	Buddhism	Feng shui
Austria															
Switzerland															
Germany															
Denmark															
Belgium															
Spa															
Health farm															
Yoga															
Buddhism															
Feng shui															
Daughter															
Husband															
Sister															
Neighbor															
Mom															

1. The sisters take a yoga class, but not in Denmark.
2. Louise is in Germany, but not to do yoga, and not with her daughter.
3. Nora is going to a health farm with her mom, but not in Austria.
4. Maureen's neighbor is taking her to Switzerland, but not to study feng shui.
5. The spa is in Belgium. Brenda isn't going there.

127 DIFFICULTY ✪✪✪✪✪✪✪✪✪  Minutes

On Princess Pargetta's twenty-first birthday, five world leaders gave her lavish gifts. Can you figure out which VIPs from which countries gave what?

1. King Aroo gave her a silver ring.
2. The blue yacht came from Habalor.
3. The Emperor of Karajan's gift was gold.
4. The black horse came from a country beginning with "B" and was not given by a prince.
5. Rup from Belon did not give a living gift, but the sultan did.
6. Prince Pia's gift couldn't talk, like Hoi's.

	Yol	Rup	Pia	Aroo	Hol	Ring	Horse	Yacht	Ferrari	Parrot	Belon	Bahrat	Karajan	Habalor	Najima	Gold	Silver	Bronze	Black	Blue
Sultan																				
King																					
Prince																					
President																					
Emperor																					
Gold																					
Silver																					
Bronze																					
Black																					
Blue																					
Belon																					
Bahrat																					
Karajan																					
Habalor																					
Najima																					
Ring																					
Horse																					
Yacht																					
Ferrari																					
Parrot																					

128 DIFFICULTY ✪✪✪✪✪✪✪✪✪✪  6 Minutes

Each row and column contains the same numbers and signs, but they are arranged in a different order each time. Find the correct order to arrive at the final totals shown.

14	**+**	**22**	**X**	**11**	**−**	**34**	**=**	**362**
							=	**630**
							=	**142**
							=	**751**
=		**=**		**=**		**=**		
465		**428**		**222**		**451**		

129 DIFFICULTY ✪✪✪☆☆☆☆☆☆☆

3 Minutes

The number 16,793 appears just once in this grid and occurs in a straight line, running either backward or forward in a horizontal, vertical, or diagonal direction. Can you locate it?

1	1	6	7	9	1	6	1	6	3	9
1	7	7	9	3	9	6	3	1	7	3
9	1	6	6	3	9	9	7	6	7	9
7	3	7	9	3	6	7	1	6	1	6
6	6	7	6	3	9	6	7	9	3	1
1	6	7	6	3	7	3	3	7	7	7
6	7	3	9	9	1	9	6	3	9	6
7	7	6	3	6	6	6	9	6	6	9
1	6	7	9	9	3	7	6	1	9	3
7	1	3	6	3	9	6	7	1	7	9
9	1	7	3	1	1	6	1	3	1	6

130 DIFFICULTY ✪✪✪✪✪✪✪✪✩✩

2 Minutes

Study this picture of large and small flowers for two minutes, then see if you can answer the questions on page 104.

131 DIFFICULTY ✪✪✪✪✪✪✪✩✩✩

2 Minutes

Study this flag for two minutes, then see if you can answer the questions on page 104.

[130] DIFFICULTY ✪✪✪✪✪✪✪✪☆☆

Can you answer these questions about the puzzle on page 103 without looking back?

1. How many large flowers appear?
2. How many small flowers appear?
3. How many large flowers have red inner petals and blue outer petals?
4. How many small flowers have orange outer petals and blue inner petals?
5. Which are the more numerous: large flowers with red outer petals or small flowers with red inner petals?
6. All the flowers have the same number of outer and inner petals; what is the total number of outer and inner petals on each flower?
7. How many large flowers have blue inner petals?
8. How many flowers have outer petals of the same color as the inner petals?

[131] DIFFICULTY ✪✪✪✪✪✪✪☆☆☆

Can you answer these questions about the puzzle on page 103 without looking back?

1. Which shape appears most often on the flag?
2. How many triangles appear on the flag?
3. How many circles appear on the pink section of the flag?
4. Not including the sections of the flag, how many shapes are there in total?
5. How many red stars have yellow borders?
6. What color is the section at the bottom left of the flag?
7. What is the total number of shapes in the green section?
8. What is the total number of shapes with dark blue borders?

132 DIFFICULTY ✪✪✪✪✪✪✪☆☆☆ ⏱ 5 Minutes

Using up, down, left, and right only, a continuous loop can be drawn on this grid so that all the numbered squares contain the correct number of sides bordering it (see examples at the bottom of the page). You don't need to travel across every dot. We've started the path off for you.

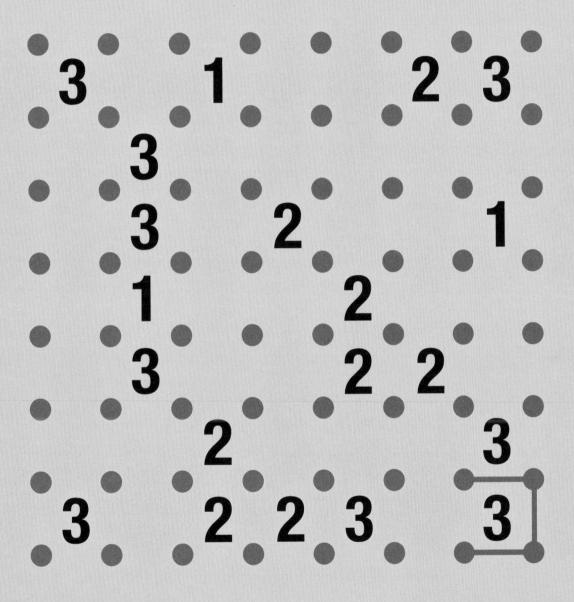

ANSWERS

1

The path is indicated in red.

2

3

Geoffrey was at the Hilton with his umbrella (clue 1). Maria lost the alarm clock (clue 2), not at the Hilton (clue 1). Maria and her alarm clock were not in room 2 or 21 (clue 2). The Royal room number is 2 (clue 3), so Maria didn't lose her alarm clock there (clue 2). Rupert was in room 33 (clue 4). The glasses were not his, or in room 33 (clue 4). Rupert didn't own the alarm clock (Maria) or the umbrella (Geoffrey). So room 33 did not hold either of these items. Rupert didn't stay at the Hilton (Geoffrey) so room 33 isn't there. The watch belongs to a woman (clue 5) and not Maria (clue 2), so it must be Caroline's. The glasses don't then belong to Caroline, or Maria (clue 2), Geoffrey (clue 1), or Rupert (clue 4), so they must be Gerald's. The camera must then belong to Rupert, and have been found in room 33 (clue 4), not at the Hilton (Geoffrey), or the Royal (clue 3).

Gerald's glasses were not in the Hilton (clue 1). Rupert's camera wasn't at the Hilton (clue 1) or the Royal (clues 3 and 4). Caroline's watch wasn't in the Novotel (clue 5). Maria's (and her alarm clock's) room number wasn't 2 or 21 (clue 2), or 33 (clue 4) or 65 (clue 6), so it must be 50, which is not then at the Hilton (clue 1). Caroline's room number (and that of her watch) is higher than Maria's (clue 6), so must be 65. So Geoffrey's umbrella wasn't in room 65, nor was it in rooms 33 (clue 4), 50 (Maria's alarm clock), or 2— which belonged to the Royal (clue 3) and we know Geoffrey stayed at the Hilton (clue 1)—so it must have been in room 21. This leaves room 2 (at the Royal, clue 3) as host to Gerald's glasses. Caroline and her watch didn't stay at the Travelodge (clue 6), the Hilton (clue 1), the Novotel (clue 5), or the Royal (Gerald's glasses), so they must have

stayed at the Westin in room 65. Maria's room, 50, and her alarm clock weren't in the Travelodge (clue 6), the Hilton (clue 1), the Royal (clue 3), or the Westin (Caroline's watch), so they must have been in the Novotel, leaving the Travelodge to Rupert and his camera. So: Geoffrey—Hilton—21—umbrella
Rupert—Travelodge—33—camera
Gerald—Royal—2—glasses
Maria—Novotel—50—alarm clock
Caroline—Westin—65—watch

4

8 ÷ 4 + 9 x 2 − 6 − 7 = 9

5

14; multiply scale a by 6 to give 6 knives + 6 forks = 24 spoons. Transpose the info from scale b into the multiplied version of scale a, thus 6 knives + 3 spoons = 24 spoons, so 6 knives = 21 spoons or 2 knives = 7 spoons. Thus 14 spoons are needed to balance scale c.

6

2	7	3	5	8	4	9	1	6
1	6	8	9	3	2	7	4	5
4	9	5	1	6	7	2	3	8
5	8	4	7	2	9	3	6	1
7	1	2	3	4	6	5	8	9
6	3	9	8	1	5	4	2	7
8	5	1	4	9	3	6	7	2
9	4	6	2	7	1	8	5	3
3	2	7	6	5	8	1	9	4

7

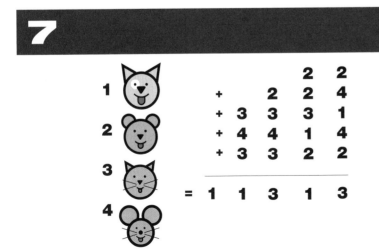

8

2	3	2	7	7	2	7	2	5	4	3	2
7	3	4	2	3	4	6	5	7	3	3	7
2	7	2	4	2	5	6	7	2	4	4	2
2	3	5	5	3	3	6	5	5	7	3	7
2	5	2	4	4	4	4	7	4	4	3	6
7	3	7	5	3	3	2	5	5	3	2	5
6	5	6	2	2	2	3	7	6	4	2	4
5	7	3	2	3	3	6	6	3	6	3	3
3	2	5	5	3	5	4	2	5	5	2	2
4	5	4	4	5	6	5	4	4	4	4	2
2	3	7	5	3	7	3	6	2	3	3	7
2	3	4	5	6	2	7	3	2	7	2	2

9

4	x	5	−	8	+	2	=	14
x			−		+		x	
8	−	4	x	2	+	5	=	13
−			+		−		−	
5	+	2	x	4	−	8	=	20
+			x		x		+	
2	x	8	+	5	−	4	=	17
=			=		=		=	
29		24		30		6		

10

d; each shape has a big outer purple circle and a smaller inner purple circle. In addition, each vertical and horizontal line contains one shape with a small blue inner square, one with a small white inner square, and one with a small purple inner square. Each vertical and horizontal line also contains one shape with a larger blue square, one with a larger white square, and one with a larger purple square. The missing shape must contain a small blue inner square and a larger blue square.

11

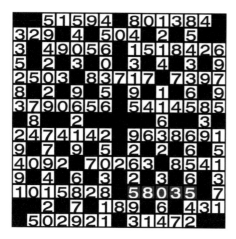

12

24714; in all the others, the first three digits added together equal the number formed by the last two digits e.g., 7 + 8 + 4 = 19 (78419).

13

a; one is a mirror image of the other.

14

5 X 4 ÷ 2 − 8 + 6 − 3 = 5

15

6	7	8	5	4	9	1	3	2
2	9	3	6	1	7	4	8	5
4	1	5	2	8	3	9	6	7
3	8	2	7	9	6	5	1	4
5	6	1	4	2	8	7	9	3
7	4	9	3	5	1	8	2	6
9	3	6	8	7	5	2	4	1
8	2	7	1	6	4	3	5	9
1	5	4	9	3	2	6	7	8

16

Zak is Zak Carlisle and he was in the hog tie. He wasn't 4th or 5th and wasn't in the meadow (1). The 3rd place was in the church house, and wasn't Amy or Betty Lou (2). The 4th place in the lasso wasn't Amy or Betty Lou or a Grady (3). The pie eater wasn't a Grady or 5th. The pumpkin thrower wasn't 1st (4). The pie eating was not in the barn or the church house (5). Amy was in the yard, and was not Smith or Carlisle (6). Betty Lou is Betty Lou McClusky, was not 1st, and was not in the lasso or competing in the barn (7). Shooter was 1st, not in hog tie or pie eating, and not in the barn or church house (8). The pumpkin thrower in the town square was a woman (9), and so must be Betty Lou McClusky, as Amy was in the yard (6). Shooter wasn't in the barn, the church house (8), the town square (Betty Lou), or the yard (Amy), so he must have been 1st (8) in the meadow. Shooter wasn't in the pie eating (8), so it wasn't in the meadow. The pie eating wasn't in the barn or church house (5), or the town square (9), so it must have been in the yard with Amy (6). The pie eating wasn't Grady (4), Carlisle (1), or McClusky (Betty the pumpkin thrower), and Amy isn't a Smith

(6), so she must be Amy Denton. Amy Denton the pie eater wasn't 1st (8), 3rd (2), 4th (3), or 5th (4), so she must have been 2nd. Zak wasn't 1st (8), 2nd (Amy), or 4th or 5th (1), so he must have been 3rd. Betty Lou McClusky, the town square pumpkin thrower, wasn't 1st (8), 2nd (Amy), 3rd (Zak), or 4th (3), so she must have been 5th. 4th place didn't go to McClusky (Betty Lou, 5th), Grady (3), Denton (Amy, 2nd) or Carlisle (1), so it must have gone to (Johnny) Smith. Shooter isn't a Smith (Johnny) or a McClusky (7), Denton (Amy), or Carlisle (1), so he must be a Grady. Zak Carlisle wasn't 4th or 5th (1), 1st (Shooter Grady), or 2nd (Amy Denton), so he must have been 3rd, in the hog tie (1) in the church house (2), leaving the barn to Johnny Smith, the 4th-place lassoer, and line dancing to Shooter. So:

Zak—Carlisle—hog tie—Church House—3rd

Shooter—Grady—line dancing—Meadow—1st

Betty Lou—McClusky—pumpkin throwing—Town Square—5th

Johnny—Smith—Lasso—Barn—4th

Amy—Denton—pie eating—Yard—2nd

17

18

4	X	3	–	6	+	2	=	8
X		+		+		X		
2	+	4	–	3	x	6	=	18
+		–		–		–		
3	+	6	x	2	–	4	=	14
–		X		X		+		
6	–	2	x	4	+	3	=	19
=		=		=		=		
5		2		28		11		

19

c; each vertical and horizontal line contains one shape with a central red square, one with a central white square, and one with a central green square.

Each vertical and horizontal line also contains one shape with a black dot on the left, one with a black dot on the right, and one with no black dot. The missing shape should have a central red square and no black dot.

20

7935; the rest are in pairs whereby the fourth and second digits are followed by the third and first digits, i.e., 9364/4369, 5973/3975, 7851/1857, 6872/2876.

21

b; looking across lines progress +3, −1, +3. Looking down lines progress +1, −3, +1.

22

944; deduct 11, 13, 15, 17, 19, 21.

23

Gavin made the crumble for Tables (1). Delish had the chocolate dish, and not a tart or cake. The pie was apple, not made by Sally or Rachel (2). The cake was not made by Pierre, Gavin, or Arthur (2). Pierre made the banana dish, not for YumYum or Din (4). The rhubarb dish was made for Din, not by Sally (5). Pierre's banana dish was not for YumYum or Din (4), Delish (2), or Tables (1), so it must be for Resto. The apple pie wasn't for Tables (1), Delish (2), Din (5), or Resto (Pierre's banana), so it must be for YumYum. Delish didn't have a crumble (1), tart, cake (2), or pie (YumYum), so it must have had a soufflé. Tables' crumble wasn't chocolate (2), apple (YumYum), banana (Resto), or rhubarb (5), so it must be cherry. Pierre's banana dish for Resto isn't a pie (3), a cake (3), a soufflé (Delish), or a crumble (cherry), so it must be a tart, leaving the Din's rhubarb dish to be a cake. YumYum's apple pie isn't Pierre (4), Gavin (1), or Sally or Rachel (3), so it must be Arthur. Sally's dish isn't apple (2), rhubarb (5), cherry (Gavin's crumble), or banana (4), so it must be

chocolate, leaving Rachel to have made Din's rhubarb cake. So:
Delish—Sally—Chocolate—Soufflé
Resto—Pierre—Banana—Tart
YumYum—Arthur—Apple—Pie
Tables—Gavin—Cherry—Crumble
Din—Rachel—Rhubarb—Cake

24

Code: Green = Left. Blue = Right. Yellow = Up. Red = Down.

Move the number of squares indicated by the spots on the dice.

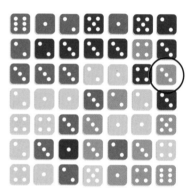

25

26

The combination is 54. Correct versions of false statements:

B. Bizet composed the opera *Carmen*.
D. The currency of Portugal is the euro.
I. George W. Bush is the 43rd President of the United States.
K. In the game of poker, a flush beats a straight.
N. The 1998 Winter Olympics were held in Nagano, Japan.

27

1. Red	4. Black	7. 3
2. Pink	5. 12	8. Green
3. Yellow	6. Blue	

28

b; the large square turns to a circle, and black dots turn to white.

29

9782; in all the others, multiply the second and fourth digits to obtain the number formed by the first and third digits, e.g., 3 x 9 = 27 (2379)

30

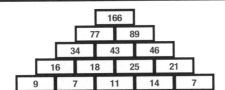

31

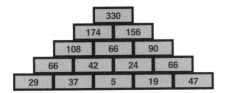

32

33

8	x	7	–	15	+	6	=	47
–		x		–		x		
7	+	8	x	6	–	15	=	75
x		+		x		+		
6	+	15	–	8	x	7	=	91
+		–		+		–		
15	–	6	x	7	+	8	=	71
=		=		=		=		
21		65		79		89		

34

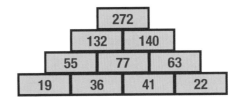

35

201; it is the seventeen times table with numbers reversed: 17, 34, 51, 68, 85, 102.

36

9 ÷ 3 x 2 + 6 + 4 − 7 = 9

37

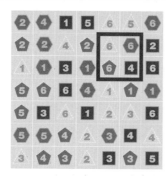

38

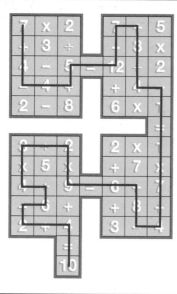

39

Svensson was not in Iceland, and didn't drive a Ford or Renault, or any blue car (1). The orange car didn't win in Britain, Spain, or with Johan (2). Sven Magnussen was not in a Renault or Subaru (3). Ford won in Iceland, and was not red (4). Mats won in Ireland, not in a Citroën or Renault (5). Gunter drove a black car, not in Italy,

and not a Seat (6). Jonsson drove a yellow car, not in Britain or Ireland, and not a Renault (7). Hankonen won in Italy, not in a Renault (8). The Spain winner was in a blue car, not a Citroën (9). Juha wasn't in a yellow car; Mats wasn't in an orange car (10). The Renault wasn't driven by Svensson (1), Magnussen (3), Hankonen (8), or Jonsson (7), so it must have been Larsson. The Irish race wasn't won by Jonsson (7), Larsson (Renault, not Ireland, 5), Magnussen (Sven 3, 5), or Hankonen (8), so it must have been (Mats) Svensson. Jonsson didn't win in Spain (blue car, not yellow, 9, 7), Italy (8), or Great Britain or Ireland (7), so he must have won in Iceland in his yellow car. Gunter didn't win in Spain in his black car (6, 9), Iceland (yellow car), Italy (6), or Ireland (5), so he must have won in Britain. Sven Magnussen didn't then win in Britain, or Iceland (Jonsson), Italy (8), or Ireland (5), so he must have won in Spain in a blue car (9), that wasn't a Renault (3), Citroën (9), Ford (4), or Subaru (3), so it must have been a Seat. Larsson's Renault didn't then win in Spain; neither did it win in Iceland (4), Italy (8), or Ireland (Svensson), so it must have won in Great Britain, and be Gunter's black car. So Mats Svensson wasn't driving the Seat (Sven Magnussen), the Renault (1), Citroën (5), or Ford (1), which leaves him the Subaru. Hankonen's Italian win (8) wasn't in the Subaru (Svensson), or the Renault (8), Ford (4), or Seat (Magnussen), so he must have driven the Citroën, leaving the Ford to Jonsson, which means the Ford was yellow and won in Iceland. Juha didn't drive the yellow car (10), neither did Gunter (6), Sven (blue), or Mats (Svensson, not Jonsson, 7), so it must have been Johan, who must then be Johan Jonsson, so the yellow car is his Ford. Mats didn't drive an orange car (10), so his must have been a red Subaru, leaving Juha the orange Citroën, and making him Juha Hankonen. So:

Gunter Larsson—Britain—Black Renault
Johan Jonsson—Iceland—Yellow Ford
Sven Magnussen—Spain—Blue Seat
Juha Hankonen—Italy—Orange Citroën
Mats Svensson—Ireland—Red Subaru

43

12	+	9	x	3	–	6	=	57
x		+		x		+		
6	x	3	+	9	–	12	=	15
–		–		+		–		
9	x	6	–	12	+	3	=	45
+		x		–		x		
3	+	12	x	6	–	9	=	81
=		=		=		=		
66		72		33		135		

40

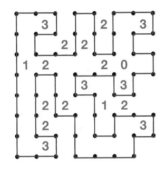

44

41

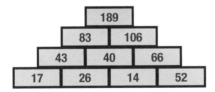

42

1	4	2	2	1	3	3	2
3	6	5	5	6	0	0	5
3	5	5	0	3	2	0	0
5	4	1	1	1	4	5	3
5	0	6	1	0	1	6	6
4	6	3	0	6	2	2	2
1	4	3	2	6	4	4	4

45

12; since 1 blue ball = 1 red ball and 8 green balls (scale B), replace the blue ball in scale A with 1 red and 8 green balls, so that there are 4 red and 8 green balls balancing 12 green balls in scale A; thus 4 red balls = 4 green balls, so 1 red = 1 green ball. Now use this in scale B; thus 1 blue ball = 1 green ball + 8 green balls, so 1 blue ball = 9 green balls. Therefore, in scale C there would be 12 green balls and, since 1 green = 1 red, 12 red balls are needed to balance scale C.

46

486; in all the others, take the square of the middle digit to obtain the number formed by the first and third digits, i.e., $7^2 = 49$ (479)

47

93, 8; there are two interwoven sequences: + 23 starting at 1 and − 23 starting at 100.

48

7 − 2 x 4 + 8 − 3 ÷ 5 = 5

49

6	8	4	2	3	5	9	1	7
1	3	7	6	9	4	5	8	2
5	2	9	7	1	8	6	4	3
8	4	1	5	7	3	2	9	6
7	5	2	9	8	6	1	3	4
3	9	6	1	4	2	8	7	5
4	6	8	3	5	9	7	2	1
2	7	3	8	6	1	4	5	9
9	1	5	4	2	7	3	6	8

50

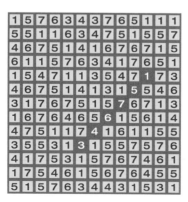

51

The combination is 87. Correct versions of false statements:
E. James T. Kirk's middle name is Tiberius.
H. There is one even prime number (2).
K. The Panama Canal is 51 miles long.
N. Kahlua is a coffee-flavored liqueur.

52

7	1	8	6	4		4	3	1	5	8	6
1	9	8		4		4	1	0		7		2
6		1	0	3	5	1		1	2	1	1	6	6	4
9		4		4		0		2		9		1		2
2	2	9	3		6	7	4	9	1		6	2	9	7
9		0		8		2		5		2		4		8
5	7	3	6	5	3		2	3	1	3	3	9	4
	6		4				8			3
7	3	3	2	9	7	6		9	5	2	9	1	2	5
4		9		3		5		1		7		8		1
7	8	6	9		5	5	0	2	2		3	1	2	2
1		6		4		1		3		5		4		9
3	1	3	2	6	5	4		4	9	7	7	7		1
	4		4		8	3	5		5		6	1	6
6	3	8	9	1	4		3	5	3	7	2

53

d; all the other boxes are mirror images of the box above or to the side, except that the two closest digits increase by 1 from left to right and top to bottom, and the digits farthest away reduce by 1.

54

The digits top left progress 7, 6, 5, 4. The digits top right progress 15, 11, 7, 3. The digits bottom left progress 2, 5, 8, 11. The digits bottom right progress 6, 13, 20, 27.

4	3
11	27

55

39574; reverse the previous number each time and subtract 1 from the middle digit.

56

d; the square on the left goes to the bottom, the square on the right goes to the top left, and the square in the middle goes to the top right.

57

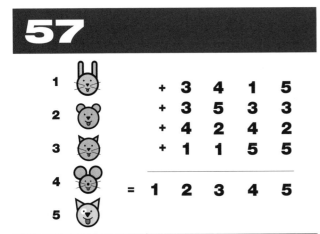

58

d; dots transfer from inside to outside of the pentagon and vice versa, and dots change from blue to white and vice versa.

59

31; starting at 1 and work clockwise, jumping over one segment each time, add 2, 4, 6, 8, 10, 12.

60

Using standard techniques, you can deduce a certain amount of information as shown. Note that the small blocks simply inherit the number of the block on which they lie:

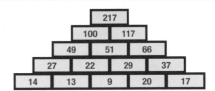

This leaves one missing number. Let's call this X and work upward, as illustrated. We can see that 68 is the sum of X+23 and X+27, i.e., 68 = 2X+50. This simplifies to 2X = 18, hence X=9. From here it is straightforward to complete the rest of the pyramid:

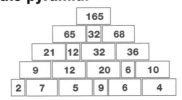

61

62

c; in all the others, the number formed by the top two digits multiplied by 3 equals the number formed by the bottom three digits, e.g., 84 x 3 = 252. In c: 37 x 4 = 148.

63

64

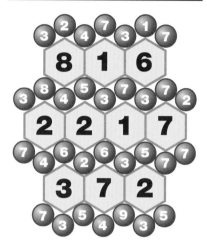

67

		196		
	92		104	
44		48		56
27	17		31	25

68

195; the digits 95273861 are being repeated in the same order.

65

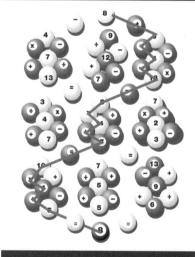

69

41648; in all the others, multiply the first digit by 3 to obtain the number formed by the second and third digits, then multiply the number formed by the second and third digits by 4 to obtain the number formed by the remaining digits. For example: 8 x 3 = 24 and 24 x 4 = 96 (82496). In 41648, multiply by 4 and 3 respectively, instead of 3 and 4.

70

52 + 27 − 34 ÷ 9 x 19 + 66 = 161

66

71

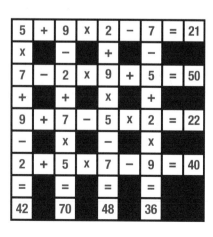

72

a; each vertical and horizontal line contains two orange tiles and a purple one. Each vertical and horizontal line contains a cracked tile and two unbroken ones. Each vertical and horizontal line contains a vase with a white collar, a vase with a blue collar, and a vase with a yellow collar. Each vertical and horizontal line contains two flowers with two leaves and one with one leaf. Each vertical and horizontal line contains two vases with a white zigzag at the waist and one where the zigzag is blue. Each vertical and horizontal line contains one tile that is the right way up, one turned 90 degrees left, and one turned 90 degrees right. The missing tile should be orange and unbroken with a white collar, two leaves, a blue zigzag at the waist, and it should be the right way up.

73

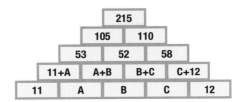

The top three levels are straightforward. For the other numbers, we need to employ a different approach. One method is to replace the three unknowns with the letters A, B, and C. This gives us these three equations:

$53 = (11+A) + (A+B)$, hence $2A+B = 42$.
$52 = (A+B) + (B+C)$, hence $A+2B + C = 52$.
$58 = (B+C) + (C+12)$, hence $B+2C = 46$.

Adding the first and last equation together gives: $2A + 2B + 2C = 88$, hence $A + B + C = 44$.

Comparing this to the middle equation shows that B must be 8, since it has another B and its total is 8 higher. Now that we know B = 8, it's easy to see that A = 17 and C = 19 from the other equations. The rest of the pyramid can now be completed:

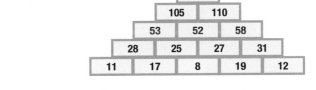

74

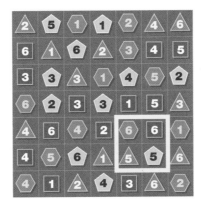

75

1. F
2. White
3. W
4. C
5. 4
6. 31
7. Q
8. 14

76

27; each triangle contains the difference given by the two-digit number in the corner circles on its horizontal side and the number in the circle opposite. So the missing number is 33 − 6 = 27.

77

39 ÷ 13 x 64 − 47 + 59 ÷ 12 = 17

78

79

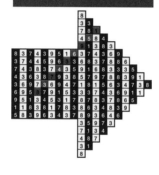

80

a; the line goes inside the circle it is attached to, and the circle on the opposite corner reduces in size and goes in the middle of the circle with the line.

81

82

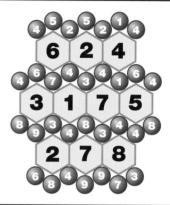

83

84

The combination is 34. Correct versions of false statements:

B. On the stock market, a stag buys new share issues hoping to make a profit.

C. The American War of 1812 ended in 1815.

I. Testa Rossa is a famous model of Ferrari car.

K. Pathophobia is the fear of disease.

N. Charles Dickens wrote under the pen name of Boz.

85

31 + 17 − 15 x 3 ÷ 9 + 42 = 53

86

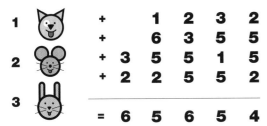

1	
2	
3	
4	
5	
6	

```
+       1  2  3  2
+       6  3  5  5
+    3  5  5  1  5
+    2  2  5  5  2
_____
=    6  5  6  5  4
```

87

128; multiply all the digits in each number to obtain the next number in the sequence.

88

b; looking across, lines progress +3, +4, +5. Looking down, lines progress −1, −2, −3.

89

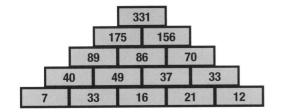

331
175 156
89 86 70
40 49 37 33
7 33 16 21 12

90

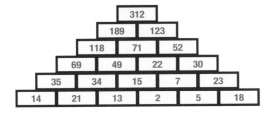

312
189 123
118 71 52
69 49 22 30
35 34 15 7 23
14 21 13 2 5 18

91

92

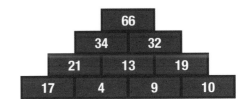

```
0  4  2  1  4  1
2  3  2  4  1  1
1  2  0  2  3  3
2  4  3  0  1  0
4  4  3  3  0  0
```

93

```
        66
      34  32
    21  13  19
  17   4   9  10
```

94

13	x	2	−	6	+	9	=	29
−		x		x		+		
9	−	6	x	13	+	2	=	41
+		+		+		x		
2	x	13	−	9	+	6	=	23
x		−		−		−		
6	x	9	+	2	−	13	=	43
=		=		=		=		
36		16		85		53		

95

| 16 | x | 4 | + | 20 | ÷ | 6 | + | 37 | − | 8 | = | 43 |

96

1438; all the others proceed +5, −1, +3; i.e., 7 (+5) = 12 (−1) = 11 (+3) = 14 to produce the number 7121114.

97

98

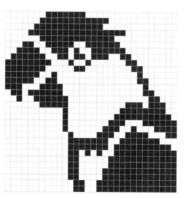

99

100

The combination is 20. Correct versions of false statements:
C. The unit of frequency is called the Hertz.
H. Matthias was the apostle who replaced Judas.
J. Jupiter is the largest planet in the solar system.

101

Steve is Steve Stone, he won in Paris, not with a royal flush (1). Lopez's nickname is "Animal," he won with a full house (2). The "Tornado" won in Vegas, not with three kings or ace high (3). Simon won with two pairs, not in London or Reno (4). Barry's nickname is "Top Hat"; he didn't win in Monte Carlo (5). Julie is Julie Kelly; she didn't win in Vegas or with a royal flush (6). Reno was won with three kings, not by "Raiser" (7). Steve Stone didn't win in Paris with a full house (2), a royal flush (1), two pairs (4), or three kings (7), so he must have won with ace high. Jackson didn't win in Vegas (8) and neither did Kelly (6), "Animal" Lopez (3), or Stone (1), so it must have been Foster, and he must be the "Tornado." Julie Kelly didn't win with a full house (2), a royal flush (6), two pairs (4), or ace high (Steve Stone), so it must have been with three kings at Reno. The full house wasn't then Julie, or Steve Stone (2), Barry "Top Hat" (2), or Simon (4), so it must have been Dave, who must then be Dave "Animal" Lopez. Vegas-winning Foster the "Tornado" isn't Dave Lopez (2), Steve (1), Julie (6), or Barry (5), so he must be Simon, winning with two pairs. The royal flush wasn't Simon Foster, or Kelly (6), Lopez (2), or Stone (1), so it must have been Jackson. Jackson isn't Dave (Lopez), Steve (1), Julie (6), or Simon (Foster), so it must be Barry "Top Hat." Barry "Top Hat" Jackson's royal flush didn't win in Vegas (8), Reno (7), Paris (1), or Monte Carlo (5), so it must have been in London, leaving Dave "Animal" Lopez with Monte Carlo. "Raiser" didn't win with a full house (2), royal flush ("Top Hat"), two pairs ("Tornado"), or three kings (7), so it must have been with ace high, and be Steve Stone, making Julie Kelly "Riches." So:

Dave "Animal" Lopez—full house—
    Monte Carlo
Steve "Raiser" Stone—ace high—Paris
Julie "Riches" Kelly—three kings—Reno
Barry "Top Hat" Jackson—royal flush—
    London
Simon "Tornado" Foster—two pairs—
    Vegas

102

2; multiply scale B by 3, thus 3 bananas + 3 plums = 15 cherries. From scale A, 1 banana + 1 cherry = 3 plums. Transpose this info into the revised scale B, thus 3 bananas + 1 banana + 1 cherry = 15 cherries, so 4 bananas = 14 cherries and 2 bananas = 7 cherries. Multiply scale B by 2, thus 2 bananas + 2 plums = 10 cherries. Replace 2 bananas with 7 cherries on this scale, thus 7 cherries + 2 plums = 10 cherries, so 2 plums = 3 cherries. Thus scale C is 3 cherries + 4 cherries = 7 cherries = 2 bananas.

103

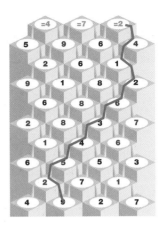

104

105

24 ÷ 6 x 9 + 14 − 11 x 2 = 78

106

11 − 4 x 12 ÷ 6 + 7 + 10 = 31

107

The digits crossed by a zigzag from bottom left progress by −2, i.e., 10, 8, 6, 4, 2. The digits crossed by a zigzag from top left progress by +4, i.e., 1, 5, 9, 13, 17.

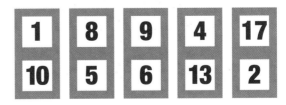

108

2	3	5	9	7	1	6	4	8
7	4	1	8	5	6	2	9	3
8	6	9	2	3	4	7	5	1
9	7	3	6	8	5	4	1	2
6	1	4	7	9	2	8	3	5
5	2	8	4	1	3	9	7	6
4	5	2	1	6	7	3	8	9
3	9	6	5	4	8	1	2	7
1	8	7	3	2	9	5	6	4

109

b; each vertical and horizontal line contains one shape with two stars, one with three, and one with four. Each vertical and horizontal line also contains one shape with a blue moon, one with an orange moon, and one with a white moon. Each vertical and horizontal line also contains one black sky and two blue ones, and each vertical and horizontal line contains one moon pointing right and two pointing left. The missing shape should contain four stars and a blue sky, and the moon should be white and facing right.

110

6	2	5	2	4		7	6	5	3	8	2
4	6	2		9		4	1	0		2		1
2		8	7	0	2	7		4	7	4	3	2	0	3
6		3		2		2		2		3		0		5
3	1	7	0		6	9	5	9	3		2	6	8	2
9		6		3		2		2		8		4
8	2	7	1	9	7	5		6	3	1	9	0	8	3
	8			5				3			7
5	3	4	1	2	7	3		3	3	8	0	5	1	4
7		8		0		2		7		8		7		0
3	5	6	8		5	0	4	1	6		2	4	8	4
2		8		9		5		4		9		6		1
7	3	9	1	2	7	4		2	5	6	1	4	2
	1		0		2	8	6		7		8	7	5
	7	3	1	9	3	5		8	6	9	2	0

111

112

$$46 \times 13 - 94 \div 36 + 39 \times 4 = 212$$

113

Billy bought a handful of lemon drops, not at the supermarket (1). Toffee wasn't bought in a quantity of two, or by Danny or Amy (2). Titch got aniseed balls from the Tuck Shop (3). Toffee wasn't bought by Billy (1), Amy (2), Danny (2), or Titch (3), so they must be for Milly. Candyland sells toffee, not by the bag or handful (4), so Milly went there. The supermarket doesn't sell two of anything. Amy didn't go there (5), neither did Billy (1), Milly (Candyland), or Titch (Tuck Shop, 3) so Danny must have gone there. Watson's sells by the pound, but not chocolate whirls (6). Watson's pound wasn't of toffee (4), aniseed balls (3), lemon drops (1), or chocolate whirls (6), so it must have been of licorice. Milly's toffees from Candyland weren't sold in a bag or handful (4), a pound (6), or two (2), so the quantity must have been five. The supermarket didn't sell by the pound (6), the handful (1), five (Candyland), or two (5), so it must have sold the bag. The Tuck Shop didn't then sell Titch a bag of aniseed balls, or a pound (6), a handful (1), or five (Candyland), so it must have sold him two, leaving the handful (Billy's lemon drops) to the Cabin. Amy didn't go to the Tuck Shop (3), the supermarket (5), the Cabin (Billy), or Candyland (Milly), so she went to Watson's for the pound of licorice. Danny didn't buy toffees (2), licorice (Amy), aniseed balls (3), or lemon drops (1), so he bought chocolate whirls (by the bag from the supermarket). So:

Amy—Watson's—Pound of Licorice
Billy—The Cabin—Handful of Lemon Drops
Danny—Supermarket—Bag of Chocolate Whirls
Titch—Tuck Shop—Two Aniseed Balls
Milly—Candyland—Five Toffees

114

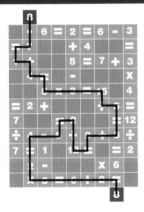

115

1	2	3	4	5	1	2	3	4	5	6	1	5	1	6
3	2	1	4	6	5	4	3	2	5	5	4	2	6	5
2	5	3	2	1	4	4	5	4	4	3	3	2	5	1
4	1	5	4	3	3	5	1	4	2	4	1	1	2	5
5	4	2	1	5	2	2	6	1	5	1	5	3	2	6
6	3	4	3	3	1	6	3	4	2	5	4	6	1	4
1	5	2	2	1	6	2	3	4	4	6	1	2	1	3
6	2	4	1	5	2	2	3	6	5	4	3	3	1	1
4	1	3	4	1	3	1	4	6	6	2	3	2	3	1
5	3	3	3	4	6	5	4	2	5	1	4	2	3	2
6	2	3	1	5	2	3	2	5	4	5	5	1	4	3
1	2	1	3	2	2	1	3	2	3	4	6	6	6	5
1	1	4	2	1	4	2	4	5	2	2	3	4	5	4
3	2	1	5	2	1	5	6	3	1	6	1	2	5	5
1	3	4	5	6	1	5	6	2	3	4	5	6	1	6

116

31	+	16	x	12	−	23	=	541
+		−		x		+		
23	−	12	x	16	+	31	=	207
−		x		+		x		
16	x	23	+	31	−	12	=	387
x		+		−		−		
12	+	31	−	23	x	16	=	320
=		=		=		=		
456		123		200		632		

117

9	8	3	1	7	2	4	6	5
2	1	4	3	5	6	8	9	7
6	7	5	8	9	4	1	2	3
1	4	9	2	8	7	5	3	6
3	2	7	5	6	1	9	4	8
8	5	6	9	4	3	7	1	2
5	6	1	4	3	8	2	7	9
4	3	8	7	2	9	6	5	1
7	9	2	6	1	5	3	8	4

118

b; a line is added to the bottom right of the first figure, a line is removed from the middle of the second figure, and a line is added to the bottom of the third figure.

119

c; each vertical and horizontal line contains two red hexagons and one white hexagon. Each vertical and horizontal line contains two hexagons with a purple border and one with no border. Each vertical and horizontal line contains a red triangle, a pink triangle, and a white triangle. Each vertical and horizontal line contains a red dot, a yellow dot, and a white dot. The missing shape should be a red hexagon with a purple border, a red triangle, and a red dot.

120

121

```
        0 7 5
      7 6 6 8 1
  3 2 1 8 8 7 3 6 4
      7 7 0 6 9 8 9
6 6 9 8 8 7 3 7 3 7 8
1 1 2 3 4 3 3 7 9 0 9 8 3
5 5 7 7 0 2 6 9 9 5 4 1 0 3 9
  0 8 8 7 8 9 1 6 3 8 6
  7 4 2 1 3 4 1 2 0 2 0 1 7
6 1 8 9 8 9 6 7 8 1 7 0 2 6 8
1 9 0 3 2 9 7 4 3 1 6 7 8 8 3 4 3
5 4 1 0 2 6 9 3 0 4 1 8 7 8 3 4 0 2 6
    7 5 4 1 0 9 5 4 1 0 2 6 9
6 9 8 8 9 0 1 4 0 2 6 7 4 6 9
1 5 4 1 0 2 6 9 5 4 1 0 2 4 9 2 6
5 4 1 0 2 6 9 1 8 6 4 5 4 1 0 2 6 6 9
          1 0 2 9 7
          4 9 2 7 3
          5 4 1 0 2
```

122

Code: move from a blank circle to a completed picture (or the other way round) one step at a time.

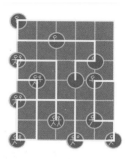

123

$$53 - 23 \times 16 - 66 \div 18 + 87 = 110$$

124

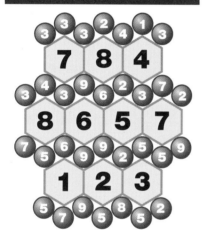

125

The bottom row should read 3, 12, 7. The left and right columns are made by doubling the number above (if there is one) and then adding together the digits of the answer (so, 6 x 2 = 12; 1 + 2 = 3, or just 2 x 2 = 4). The middle column is made by multiplying the numbers on each side and then reversing the digits.

126

The sisters are going to do yoga, not in Denmark (1). Louise is going to Germany, not for yoga, not with her daughter (2). Nora is going to the health farm with her mom, but not in Austria (3). Maureen is going with her neighbor to Switzerland, not for feng shui (4). The spa is in Belgium, but Brenda isn't going there (5). The Belgian spa visitor isn't then Brenda (5), Maureen (4), Louise (2), or Nora (3), so must be Dierdre. Nora's health farm isn't in Austria (3), Switzerland (4), Belgium (5), or Germany (2), so it must be in Denmark. Brenda isn't going to Denmark, or Belgium (5), Germany (2), or Switzerland (4), so she must be off to Austria. The yoga visitor going away with her sister isn't Maureen (4), Dierdre (spa), Louise (2), or Nora (3), so it must be Brenda. The daughter then isn't going with Brenda, Maureen (4), Louise (2), or Nora (3), so she is going with Dierdre to the Belgian spa. The husband then isn't going to Belgium, or to Austria (sister), Switzerland (4), or Denmark (mom), so he is off to Germany with Louise. Maureen and her neighbor aren't going to Switzerland for a spa (5), health farm (3), yoga (1), or feng shui (4), so they must be going to a Buddhist retreat, leaving Louise and her husband the feng shui. So:
Brenda—Austria—Sister—Yoga
Louise—Germany—Husband—Feng Shui
Nora—Denmark—Mom—Health Farm
Dierdre—Belgium—Daughter—Spa
Maureen—Switzerland—Neighbor—Buddhism

127

Aroo is the king and gave a silver ring (1). The yacht was blue and from Habalor (2). The emperor is from Karajan and gave a gold gift (3). The black gift, a horse, was not from Karajan, Habalor, or Najima (4). The horse and parrot did not come from Rup or from Belon, and the sultan's gift wasn't the ring, yacht, or Ferrari (5). Pia is the prince and Hoi's gift was the parrot (6). Rup from Belon didn't give the ring (1), horse or parrot (5), or yacht (2), so he must have given the Ferrari. Rup from Belon's Ferrari isn't gold (3), silver (1), black (4), or blue (2), so it must be bronze. The gift from Najima isn't gold (3), bronze (Belon), black (4), or blue (2), so it must be the silver ring from King Aroo. The black horse isn't from Belon (bronze), Karajan, Habalor, or Najima (4), so it must be from Bahrat. Hoi's parrot isn't from Belon (5), Bahrat (horse), Habalor (2), or Najima (ring), so it must be from Karajan and be gold (3), and Hoi must then be the Emperor of Karajan (3). The sultan's gift wasn't the ring, yacht, or Ferrari (5), or the parrot (emperor) so it must be the black horse from Bahrat. Prince Pia's gift wasn't the ring (1), horse (sultan), Ferrari (Rup), or parrot (Hoi), so it must be the blue yacht from Habalor. Rup from Belon's bronze Ferrari wasn't from a sultan (5), a king (1), a prince (6), or an emperor (3), so Rup must be president, leaving Yol as the sultan. So:

Sultan Yol of Bahrat—
  Black Horse
King Aroo of Najima—
  Silver Ring
Prince Pia of Habalor—
  Blue Yacht
President Rup of Belon—
  Bronze Ferrari
Emperor Hoi of Karajan—
  Gold Parrot

129

1	1	6	7	9	1	6	1	6	3	9
1	7	7	9	3	9	6	3	1	7	3
9	1	6	6	3	9	9	7	6	7	9
7	3	7	9	3	6	7	1	6	1	6
6	6	7	6	3	9	6	7	9	3	1
1	6	7	6	3	7	3	3	7	7	7
6	7	3	9	9	1	9	6	3	9	6
7	7	6	3	6	6	6	9	6	6	9
1	6	7	9	9	3	7	6	1	9	3
7	1	3	6	3	9	6	7	1	7	9
9	1	7	3	1	1	6	1	3	1	6

130

1. 12
2. 10
3. 5
4. 4
5. Large flowers with red outer petals
6. 12
7. None
8. 1

131

1. Circle
2. 3
3. 1
4. 16
5. 3
6. Red
7. 3
8. 5

128

14	+	22	x	11	−	34	=	362
x		+		x		−		
34	−	11	+	22	x	14	=	630
+		x		+		x		
11	x	14	−	34	+	22	=	142
−		−		-		+		
22	x	34	+	14	−	11	=	751
=		=		=		=		
465		428		222		451		

132

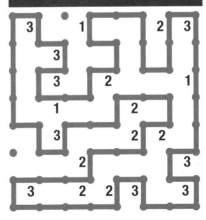

ACKNOWLEDGMENTS ✪ DEVIOUS DEDUCTIONS

✪ Puzzle contributors

Contributors are listed next to the numbers of the puzzles they created.

✪ David Bodycombe

Puzzles 26, 30, 31, 34, 40, 41, 42, 51, 60, 61, 67, 73, 84, 89, 90, 92, 93, 100, 132

✪ Brainwarp

Puzzles 1, 6, 15, 49, 76, 81, 108, 117, 125

✪ Guy Campbell

Puzzles 3, 7, 10, 16, 19, 23, 24, 25, 32, 37, 38, 39, 57, 64, 65, 65, 72, 74, 82, 74, 82, 86, 98, 101, 103, 109, 111, 113, 114, 119, 120, 122, 124, 126, 127

✪ Philip Carter

Puzzles 12, 13, 20, 21, 22, 28, 29, 35, 46, 47, 53, 54, 55, 56, 58, 59, 62, 68, 69, 80, 87, 88, 96, 107, 118

✪ Edward Phantera

Puzzle 44

✪ Puzzle Press Ltd

Puzzles 5, 8, 17, 27. 45, 50, 63, 75, 78, 79, 97, 99, 102, 115, 121, 129, 130, 131

✪ Probyn Puzzles

Puzzles 2, 4, 9, 11, 14, 18, 33, 36, 43, 48, 52, 66, 70, 71, 77, 83, 85, 91, 94, 95, 104, 105, 106, 110, 112, 116, 123, 128

DEVIOUS DEDUCTIONS was commissioned, edited, designed, and produced by:

Book Creation Ltd., 20 Lochaline Street, London W6 9SH, United Kingdom

Managing Director: Hal Robinson

Editor: David Popey **Art Editor:** Keith Miller

Designers: Nick Edwards and Mark Sayer **Copy Editors:** Sarah Barlow and Ali Moore